THE BEST OF KOREAN CUISINE

The Hippocrene Cookbook library

AFRICA AND OCEANIA
Best of Regional African Cooking
Traditional South African Cookery
Taste of Eritrea
Good Food from Australia

ASIA AND MIDDLE EAST
The Best of Taiwanese Cuisine
Imperial Mongolian Cooking
The Best of Regional Thai Cuisine
Japanese Home Cooking
The Best of Korean Cuisine
Egyptian Cooking
Sephardic Israeli Cuisine
Healthy South Indian Cooking
The Indian Spice Kitchen
The Cuisine of the Caucasus
  Mountains
Afghan Food and Cookery
The Art of Persian Cooking
The Art of Turkish Cooking
The Art of Uzbek Cooking

MEDITERRANEAN
Best of Greek Cuisine, Expanded
  Edition
Taste of Malta
A Spanish Family Cookbook
Tastes of North Africa

WESTERN EUROPE
Art of Dutch Cooking, Expanded
  Edition
A Belgian Cookbook
Cooking in the French Fashion
  (bilingual)
Cuisines of Portuguese Encounters
The Swiss Cookbook
The Art of Irish Cooking
Feasting Galore Irish-Style
Traditional Food from Scotland
Traditional Food from Wales
The Scottish-Irish Pub and Hearth
  Cookbook
A Treasury of Italian Cuisine
  (bilingual)

SCANDINAVIA
Best of Scandinavian Cooking
The Best of Finnish Cooking
The Best of Smorgasbord Cooking
Tastes & Tales of Norway
Icelandic Food & Cookery

CENTRAL EUROPE
All Along the Rhine
All Along the Danube
Best of Austrian Cuisine
Bavarian Cooking
The Best of Czech Cooking
The Best of Slovak Cooking
The Art of Hungarian Cooking
Hungarian Cookbook
Polish Heritage Cookery
The Best of Polish Cooking
Old Warsaw Cookbook
Old Polish Traditions
Treasury of Polish Cuisine *(bilingual)*
Poland's Gourmet Cuisine
The Polish Country Kitchen
  Cookbook

EASTERN EUROPE
Art of Lithuanian Cooking
Best of Albanian Cooking
Traditional Bulgarian Cooking
Best of Croatian Cooking
Taste of Romania
Taste of Latvia
The Best of Russian Cooking
The Best of Ukrainian Cuisine

AMERICAS
Argentina Cooks
A Taste of Haiti
A Taste of Quebec
Cooking With Cajun Women
Cooking the Caribbean Way
French Caribbean Cuisine
Mayan Cooking
The Art of Brazilian Cookery
The Art of South American Cookery
Old Havana Cookbook *(bilingual)*

THE BEST OF
KOREAN CUISINE

Karen Hulene Bartell

HIPPOCRENE BOOKS, INC.
NEW YORK

Also by Karen Hulene Bartell:

The Best of Taiwanese Cuisine
The Best of Polish Cooking

Book and jacket design by Acme Klong Design, Inc.

For more information, address:
HIPPOCRENE BOOKS, INC.
171 Madison Avenue
New York, NY 10016

ISBN 0-7818-0929-0

Cataloging-in-Publication Data available from the Library of Congress.
Printed in the United States of America.

This book is dedicated with love to my best friend, husband, and graphic designer, Peter.

Special thanks to Hee Sun Yang for her technical advice.

CONTENTS

INTRODUCTION

Seoul Food. Food is the soul of each ethnic culture, and in Korean cuisine Seoul takes on a double meaning. The food of Korea is a reflection of its climate, customs, beliefs, and history. Because of its similar cultural heritage with China and Japan, it would be easy to dismiss Korean cuisine as a subtle variation of Chinese cookery, but that would be an underestimation. Korean cuisine is unique.

Korean food has developed its own distinct flavors and cooking methods. Besides the ever-present rice, Korean recipes are more reliant on other grains, such as barley and buckwheat. The reasons are climatic and geographic. Korea is drier and more mountainous than its neighbors. As a result, a variety of other grain crops are grown, in addition to rice.

Although the main meat of China is pork, and Japan's mainstay is fish, beef is Korea's favorite entrée. Barbecued beef, short ribs, shish kebobs, ground beef, boiled beef, dried beef, beef organs, and chopped raw beef are all popular Korean dishes.

Koreans enjoy a wide variety of fish and shellfish, which are usually steamed but may be eaten raw. Fried eggs are eaten for breakfast, lunch, and dinner. Eggs are also the main ingredient of custards and pancakes.

An interesting feature of Korean cuisine is the emphasis on wild roots, fiddlehead ferns, and wild mushrooms. Ginger, chili pepper, garlic, green onions, sesame oil, soy sauce, and fermented bean paste are the primary flavorings.

Koreans take food seriously. They believe that a family's happiness depends upon the household's quality of food. They also consider food as medicine. Many herbs that westerners might interpret as medicinal are used in daily cooking. Though they do not distinguish between culinary and medicinal herbs, Koreans recognize the herbs' healing properties. The word *yak* means medicine. Any dish

7

that contains a prefix of *yak* in its name is fare that is considered healthy, such as *yak bap*, which means "sweet rice," made of glutinous rice, chestnuts, pine nuts, honey, and sesame oil.

Besides geographic, agricultural, and cultural beliefs, tradition plays a big role in Korean cuisine. Koreans believe in a correlation between the lunar calendar, the four seasons, and specific foods.

The lunar calendar has a sixty-year cycle. Within it, the Asian horoscope has twelve animal signs of Rat, Ox, Tiger, Rabbit, Dragon, Snake, Horse, Sheep, Monkey, Rooster, Dog, and Boar. Each of these twelve zodiac signs relates to an aspect of the five basic elements of Metal, Water, Wood, Fire, and Earth. As a result, every animal emblem contains five different symbols: for example, Metal Rat, Water Rat, Wood Rat, Fire Rat, and Earth Rat.

These five aspects correspond with the four seasons and the seasonal transitions. Certain foods are considered beneficial during the different seasons and their various aspects. *The Best of Korean Cuisine* attempts to blend the rich diversity of Korean cookery with the seasonal fare, holiday feasts, and auspicious foods suggested by the lunar calendar. The Asian horoscope is based on the lunar year. Find the year in which you were born during this sixty-year cycle to determine your sign.

Each of these twelve zodiac signs is combined with the five basic elements of Metal, Water, Wood, Fire, and Earth, which correspond with Spring, Summer, Autumn, Winter, and the seasonal transitions. Because of this rich tradition of observing the elements in relation to the four seasons, Koreans have a unique way of planning seasonal menus.

On that note, *jal mok kessum nida*, the Korean counterpart of *bon appetit*!

ASIAN HOROSCOPE

Rat	Ox	Tiger	Rabbit	Dragon	Snake
1900	1901	1902	1903	1904	1905
1912	1913	1914	1915	1916	1917
1924	1925	1926	1927	1928	1929
1936	1937	1938	1939	1940	1941
1948	1949	1950	1951	1952	1953
1960	1961	1962	1963	1964	1965
1972	1973	1974	1975	1976	1977
1984	1985	1986	1987	1988	1989
1996	1997	1998	1999	2000	2001
2008	2009	2010	2011	2012	2013
2020	2021	2022	2023	2024	2025

Horse	Ram	Monkey	Rooster	Dog	Boar
1906	1907	1908	1909	1910	1911
1918	1919	1920	1921	1922	1923
1930	1931	1932	1933	1934	1935
1942	1943	1944	1945	1946	1947
1954	1955	1956	1957	1958	1959
1966	1967	1968	1969	1970	1971
1978	1979	1980	1981	1982	1983
1990	1991	1992	1993	1994	1995
2002	2003	2004	2005	2006	2007
2014	2015	2016	2017	2018	2019
2026	2027	2028	2029	2030	2031

Spring

Two important Korean holidays occur in spring: Lunar New Year (*Sol-nal*) and the first full moon of the New Year (*Taeborum*). Both days are ideal times to celebrate with family or friends. Traditionally New Year's Day is the time for family reunions in Korea, and the first full moon is the time for fun with friends.

SOL-NAL OR NEW YEAR'S DAY

New Year's Day, or *Sol-nal*, is the first day of the lunar year. People bid farewell to the old year and welcome the new. Extended families gather to hold *Ch'aryei*, a memorial service for ancestors held in front of the household shrine, and perform *Saeba*, a ritual bow. *Sebae* is the traditional act of notifying ancestors of the New Year. Younger people show respect to their elders by bowing. The older generation blesses them with wishes of good health and good luck for the coming year.

Ch'aryei is held early on New Year's morning, and it includes the delicious ritual of eating *Ttok Kuk*, or Rice Cake Soup. Tradition holds that by eating a bowl of Rice Cake Soup, everyone grows a year older. After *Ch'aryei*, the family members enjoy a rich meal while reminiscing about their ancestors. The larger the meal, the more dishes tasted, the better the luck in the coming year!

Sol-nal / New Year's Brunch for Six

Rice Cake Soup (*Ttok Kuk*) – (See Earth Tiger, page 76)

Rice Cake and Dumpling Soup (*Ttok Mandu kuk*) – (See Earth Tiger, page 78)

Pickled Stuffed Cucumber (*Oi Sobaegi Kimchi*) – (See Wood Rabbit, page 89)

Mung Bean Pancakes (*Pindaettok*) – (See Water Tiger, page 70)

Frothy Banana Egg Sunrise – (See Earth Sheep, page 135)

Korean Rice Breakfast (*Kongnamul Kuk Bap*) – (See Metal Tiger, page 65)

Steamed Eggs with Anchovy – (See Earth Rabbit, page 93)

Grilled Spiced Fish (*Sen Saen Yang Jung Chang Kui*) – (See Metal Rabbit, page 84)

Steamed Rice (*Bap*) – (See Earth Dragon, page 106)

Sliced White Radish (*Muu Namul*) – (See Wood Tiger, page 73)

Cellophane Noodles and Shiitake Mushrooms (*Chap Chae*) – (See Fire Rabbit, page 90)

Tangerine Segments and Apple Slices

Persimmon Punch (*Sujonggwa*) – (See Metal Tiger, page 66)

TAEBORUM OR FIRST FULL MOON

The first full moon falls on the fifteenth day of the first lunar month. It is a public holiday known as *Taeborum* that signals the beginning of the agricultural cycle. Traditionally, Koreans rise early, breakfast on nuts, believing that hard foods strengthen the teeth, and toast the day with a wine called *kwibalki sul*, which is thought to sharpen the ears or open the ears to good news.

A holiday dish called Five-grain Rice, *Ogok bap*, which is a mixture of millet, sticky rice, black beans, sweet beans, sorghum, and dried vegetables, is prepared this day in the belief that eating it will avert a scorching summer.

Agricultural communities hold ceremonies to honor local spirits, hoping to ensure a good harvest. They hold community tug-of-wars. Kite flying, *yonnalligi*, is also a popular pastime on *Taeborum*. Kites are inscribed with the phrase *song-aek*, meaning "Good riddance to evil," or they carry the person's name, date of birth, and the phrase "Bad luck be gone. Good luck stay." After the kites are flown, they are set free to guarantee good fortune throughout the year.

At dusk, people race to the hilltops to see the full moon rising. The first person to spot it will have good fortune throughout the year. In a custom similar to the western practice of wishing upon a star, Koreans whisper their wishes to the first full moon. As it rises, the people build a bonfire called a *taljip* on the tallest hilltop and welcome the year's first full moon with the fire's rising smoke.

Taeborum

02/27/2002	03/05/2007	02/07/2012
02/16/2003	02/22/2008	02/25/2013
02/06/2004	02/10/2009	02/15/2014
02/24/2005	03/01/2010	03/06/2015
02/13/2006	02/18/2011	

Taeborum Dinner for Four

Nine-section Dish (*Kujulpan*) – (See Water Tiger, page 67)

Bean Sprout and Green Onion Salad – (See Wood Rabbit, page 88)

Spicy Crab Soup (*Doen Jang Jiege Keh*) – (See Metal Rabbit, page 83)

Pickled White Radish (*Yul Mu Kimchi*) – (See Wood Tiger, page 71)

Stir-Fried Mugwort with Ginkgo Seeds – (See Fire Tiger, page 75)

Bean-Thread Noodles with Sesame Sauce – (See Water Rabbit, page 86)

Five-grain Rice (*Ogok Bap*) – (See Water Rabbit, page 87)

Almonds, Chestnuts, Peanuts, and Walnuts

Sweet Rice (*Yak Bap*) – (See Earth Tiger, page 81)

Pound Cake with Crystallized Ginger – (See Metal Horse, page 120)

Barley Water Tea (*Bori Cha*) – (See Earth Rat, page 48)

Oolong Tea

SPRING AND WEDDINGS

With spring's arrival, Koreans scurry to the mountains and parks to enjoy vibrant displays of flowers. The popular food for this outing is *hwajon*, flower pancakes, so called because they are decorated with azaleas or other seasonal flowers. To make *hwajon*, pan-fry wontons made of sticky powdered rice. Then adorn them with edible flower petals to re-create the flower's image. Flower pancakes represent the season; use pink and white azalea blossoms in spring, gold chrysanthemums in autumn, and colorful jujubes (dried Korean dates) in winter when flowers are not as readily available. For fragrance and flavor, Koreans add aromatic green mugwort in the spring and ripe pumpkin in the autumn.

Although contemporary Korean weddings may be a blend of the old and new, the bride and groom traditionally observe *Tongnejile* and *Hapkeunle*. They share three spoonfuls of rice to represent the three meals they will take part in each day of their lives. The couple then pours Korean rice wine into *p'yojubak*, two cups made from the same gourd to symbolize their unity.

Spring Wedding Party

Cornish Hen Soup with Chestnuts (*Yong Keh Baiksuk*) (See Water Ox, page 54)

White Radish Soup (*Mu Kuk*) – (See Fire Tiger, page 74)

Pickled Daikon (*Kaktugi Kimchi*) – (See Wood Tiger, page 72)

Pickled Napa Cabbage (*Pom Kimchi*) – (See Wood Rat, page 45)

Barbecued Beef (*Bulgogi*) – (See Metal Dragon, page 98)

Barbecued Chicken Breasts (*Dak Bulgogi*) – (See Metal Dragon, page 97)

Barbecued Chitterlings and Tripe (*Yang Kobchang Gui*) – (See Metal Dragon, page 97)

Barbecued Pork (*Doeji Bulgogi*) – (See Metal Dragon, page 97)

Grilled Short Ribs (*Kalbi gui*) – (See Metal Dragon, page 100)

Sticky Rice (*Bap*) – (See Fire Ox, page 60)

Azalea Punch (*Jindalae Hwachae*) – (See Earth Ox, page 63)

Azalea Pancakes (*Jindalae Hwajun*) – (See Earth Ox, page 61)

Azalea Wine (Available in Asian supermarkets)

Fresh Assorted Fruit

Assortment of Pastries

The Best of Korean Cuisine

HANSIK OR ARBOR DAY

Hansik literally means "cold food" and occurs on the 105th day after the winter solstice, about the fifth of April. A time of renewal, the sky clears, the earth awakens, flowers blossom, and buds open. In the country, farmers begin spring planting and rice paddy irrigation. It is the time to shake off winter's doldrums, enjoy the first balmy days of spring, and celebrate life.

The tradition of eating cold food on *Hansik* originated from a Chinese legend, but since it coincides with Arbor Day, people use the opportunity to contribute to nature by planting trees. Families pack picnic lunches and make a day of it, eating among the fragrant buds and blossoms. *Kım bap*, Korean *sushi*, is the customary snack packed for the excursion. Sometimes barbecued short ribs are prepared on a portable grill. It is a day to enjoy the first stirrings of spring and spend time with loved ones.

Springtime Picnic

Bean Sprout Salad (*Sook Choo Na Mool*) — (See Water Dog, page 163)

Seafood Roll-ups (*Kim Bap*) — (See Water Dragon, page 101)

Radish Cube Kimchi (*Kkakttugi*) — (See Wood Dog, page 164)

Korean Barbecued Short Ribs (*Kalbi Gui*) — (See Fire Dog, page 165)

Crystallized Ginger (*Saeng Kang*) — (See Metal Horse, page 120)

Melon Slices

Papaya Slices

Summer

TANO

Tano occurs on the fifth day of the fifth lunar month. Traditionally, women wash their hair in water infused with, *ch'angp'o*, an herb of the calamus family that is believed to make hair shiny.

Two popular games during *Tano* are *kune* and *ssirum*. *Kune* or swinging contests consist of women or children on special trapezes, competing to see who can swing the highest and still ring a bell with a foot. *Ssirum*, a wrestling match that is a contest of strength and skill, is the most popular sport with men.

Good times call for good food. Often the meal will include longan, a sweet, seasonal fruit, similar to the lychee, with a rough outer skin and, when peeled, a soft round center like a huge grape. It is available fresh in May and early June, or you can purchase canned longan any time.

Tano Dinner

Spicy Fish Chowder (*Maewun Tang*) – (See Metal Sheep, page 127)

Chili Kimchi (*Kimchi*) – (See Water Snake, page 109)

Bellflower Root Salad (*Doraji Namul*) – (See Water Rooster, page 152)

Stir-Fried Rice Cake (*Ttok Bokkee*) – (See Earth Monkey, page 145)

Steamed Rice with Chestnuts (*Bap*) – (See Water Horse, page 123)

Stir-Fried Snow Peas and Green Beans – (See Water Sheep, page 130)

Shiitake Mushrooms and Sprouts with Cilantro – (See Water Sheep, page 131)

Seafood "Sausage" (*Sundae*) – (See Wood Sheep, page 133)

Candied Lotus Seeds – (Available in Asian supermarkets)

Crystallized Lotus Root Slices – (Available in Asian supermarkets)

Fresh Longans and Cherries

CHILWOL-CHILSUK OR KOREAN VALENTINE'S DAY

Chilwol-chilsuk occurs on the seventh day of the seventh month, usually falling in August. According to the legend, the constellations of the Herdsman and the Weaver, which are located at the far ends of the Milky Way Galaxy, meet once a year on this night. Legend says that the Herdsman and the Weaver loved each other so deeply, that the God of Heaven became angry and separated them, allowing them cross the "Silvery River" to meet only once a year.

On the seventh day of the seventh month, the magpies and crows spread their wings to make a bridge for these two stars to cross, which is called the Bridge of Ojack. Altair, the brightest star in the Eagle constellation, in the eastern part of the Milky Way, is the Herdsman, and Vega, the brightest star on the Harp constellation, is the Weaver.

On *Chilwol-chilsuk*, these two stars shine brightly overhead. Tradition holds that it is because the Herdsman and the Weaver have met. If rain falls the next morning, it is called *Chilsokmul* or the water of the seventh day. These are the tears that the Herdsman and the Weaver shed because they are separating for another year.

During this festival, eggplants and red peppers are in season, so they are traditional foods. Pumpkins, cucumbers, and Korean melons are also ripe, which is why fried pumpkin is another favorite holiday food.

Korean Valentine's Day Dinner for Two

Frosty Cucumber Soup (*Oi Naeng Kuk*) – (See Metal Snake, page 107)

Pickled Eggplant (*Kaji Kimchi*) – (See Wood Snake, page 110)

Korean Cucumber Salad (*Oee Namul Muchim*) – (See Wood Snake, page 113)

Bamboo Shoots with Carrot Sesame Dressing – (See Wood Dragon, page 104)

Pumpkin Fritters with Pine Nut Sauce – (See Earth Snake, page 117)

Stuffed Red Peppers (*Kochu Chon*) – (See Fire Snake, page 115)

Soy Sauce Dip (*Yang Nyom Jang*) – (See Fire Snake, page 116)

Korean Melon Wedges

Assorted Rice Cakes

SAMBOK

Sambok occurs after the rainy season, when the thermometer reaches into the 90s. This thirty-day period, which falls between mid-July and mid-August, is divided into three phases: *Ch'obok*, *Chungbok*, and *Malbok*. For centuries, Koreans have believed that eating hot foods during this season helps regulate their bodies' temperatures.

Sambok Dinner

Lettuce Wraps (*Sangchu Ssam*) – (See Metal Ox, page 51)

Sesame Soy Dip (*Ssam Jang*) – (See Metal Ox, page 53)

Pickled Cabbage with Ginger (*Saeng Kang Kimchi*) – (See Wood Snake, page 112)

Garlic Beef Roll-ups (*Gogi*) – (See Water Rat, page 44)

Buckwheat Noodles (*Mul Naeng Myun*) – (See Wood Ox, page 58)

Steamed Rice (*Bap*) – (See Earth Dragon, page 106)

Piquant Shark and Shellfish with Vegetables
(*Sengsun Meuntang*) – (See Wood Snake, page 114)

Assorted Pastries

Asian Pear Slices

Autumn

CH'USOK

The fifteenth day of the eighth lunar month is called *Ch'usok*, or Harvest Moon Festival. Actually observed for three days, this festival is regarded as the Korean Thanksgiving. Second only to Lunar New Years, it is observed just as enthusiastically.

Historically, harvests were attributed to the blessings of ancestors. However, Koreans still travel long distances to hold family reunions and visit the graves of loved ones. *Ch'usok* gives Koreans the opportunity to show their gratitude to ancestors by visiting ancestral tombs, making food offerings to their deceased ancestors, and trimming the graves' grass and shrubs.

After filial duties are completed, family members exchange gifts and play folk games. The games vary, depending on locality, but popular games are lion dances, *kune* or swinging contests, *ssirum* or wrestling matches, tugs of war with teams of men pulling at both ends of ropes, and *jumping seesaw*. Jumping seesaw involves women of all ages catapulting from seesaws and performing gymnastic feats such as midair somersaults.

Ch'usok Dinner

Typical foods served on *Ch'usok* are all made from the harvest. The traditional foods include freshly picked persimmons, taro, mushrooms, chestnuts, and *Songp'yon*, a crescent-shaped rice cake steamed on a layer of pine needles.

Taro Soup (*Kuk*) – (See Water Rat, page 43)

Instant Kimchi (*Mak Kimchi*) – (See Wood Boar, page 173)

Chili Breast of Duck with Honey-Glazed Taro – (See Metal Rooster, page 147)

Spiced Mushrooms (*Beuseus Doen Jang Jeege*) – (See Fire Boar, page 176)

Steamed Asparagus – (See Fire Boar, page 177)

Steamed Rice with Chestnuts (*Bap*) – (See Water Horse, page 123)

Crescent Rice Cakes (*Songp'yon*) – (See Earth Boar, page 178)

Sesame Pumpkin-Seed Brittle (*Tong Kkae*) – (See Earth Dog, page 166)

Fresh Persimmons and Apples

Roasted Chestnuts

Ginseng Tea

JUNGYANG

Jungyang occurs on the ninth day of the ninth lunar month, usually falling in October. Double-digit holidays are considered auspicious, particularly when the numbers are odd. This double-nine holiday is especially enjoyable because it celebrates the changing colors of the season. Maple trees are at their height of color. Chrysanthemums are in full bloom.

It's is a day to enjoy nature at its most beautiful. Families hike up the mountainsides to view the scarlet maple and persimmon trees. Afterward they decorate their dinner tables with the brilliantly colored leaves and fragrant bouquets of chrysanthemums. They drink chrysanthemum tea, nibble chrysanthemum pancakes, and toast the glorious season with sweet Chrysanthemum wine. What a perfect way to celebrate autumn with family and friends!

Autumn Celebration

Mung Bean Sprouts Salad (*Sukju Namul*) – (See Wood Rooster, page 155)

Pickled Daikon (*Kaktugi Kimchi*) – (See Wood Tiger, page 72)

Capon with Ginseng and Korean Dates (*SamgyeTang*) – (See Water Ox, page 56)

Rice with Mixed Vegetables (*Bibim Bap*) (See Water Rooster, page 149)

Steamed Rice (*Bap*) – (See Earth Dragon, page 106)

Sautéed Bellflower Root (*Doraji Namul*) (See Water Rooster, page 151)

Sautéed Fern Bracken (*Kosari Namul*) (See Water Rooster, page 153)

Chrysanthemum Pancakes (*Jindalae Hwajun*) – (See Earth Ox, page 62)

Chrysanthemum Wine (available in Asian supermarkets)

Chrysanthemum Tea (available in Asian supermarkets)

KIMCHI HOLIDAY

At the end of the harvest season, in November, the Koreans celebrate a kimchi holiday. Neighbors traditionally share in each
other's garden produce for the preparation of these fermented vegetables. Korean winters are long, while the growing season is short.
Historically, the harsh conditions forced people to preserve vegetables in order to survive the cold winters. Now this moist Korean
pickle is known worldwide for its subtle heat and tang.

The word *kimchi* means "sunken vegetables." Cabbages and daikon
(white radishes) are submerged in salty water and seasonings, such
as chili pepper and salted fish. It is the fermentation process that
produces kimchi's unique flavor, as well as vitamins B1, B2, B12,
and lactic acid. It's no wonder that kimchi is served at every meal.
Lactic acid aids digestion, while the pungent action of the chili
peppers also stimulates the digestive system.

Kimchi is an integral part of every Korean meal. It works equally
well as a spicy appetizer, a tangy condiment for rice and noodles,
or a piquant seasoning for any stew or sautéed vegetable.

Kimchi Cookery

Pickled White Radish (*Yul Mu Kimchi*) – (See Wood Tiger, page 71)

Chili Kimchi (*Kimchi*) – (See Water Snake, page 109)

Pickled Cabbage with Ginger (*Saeng Kang Kimchi*) – (See Wood
Snake, page 112)

Pickled Eggplant (*Kaji Kimchi*) – (See Wood Snake, page 110)

Pickled Napa Cabbage (*Pom Kimchi*) – (See Wood Rat, page 45)

Water Kimchi (*Na Bak Kimchi*) – (See Fire Monkey, page 143)

Pickled Stuffed Cucumber (*Oi Sobaegi Kimchi*) – (See Wood Rabbit, page 89)

Radish Cube Kimchi (*Kkakttugi*) – (See Wood Dog, page 164)

Pickled Daikon (*Kaktugi Kimchi*) – (See Wood Tiger, page 72)

Instant Kimchi (*Mak Kimchi*) – (See Wood Boar, page 173)

KIMCHI PARTY

Sip these refreshing vegetable and fruit drinks while preparing the cabbages and radishes or the dinner menu. Then, after the kimchi is fermenting in crocks or large glass jars, enjoy a well-earned meal!

Beverages

Grapefruit Cabbage Cooler (See Fire Sheep, page 134)

Tomato Juice Korean-Style (See Water Sheep, page 131)

Watermelon and Pineapple Juice (See Fire Sheep, page 134)

Hale n' Hearty Kale Juice (See Fire Horse, page 125)

Lemon Lettuce Cooler (See Fire Horse, page 125)

Mandarin Orange Celery Juice (See Earth Horse, page 126)

Melon Pear Nectar (See Wood Horse, page 124)

Orange Beer (See Earth Horse, page 126)

Dinner

Seaweed Soup (*Miyok Kuk*) (See Water Boar, page 171)

Grilled Chicken on a Skewer (*Kkochi Gui*) (See Metal Boar, page 169

Grilled Pollack and Scallions (*Bugo Kochuchang Gui*) – (See Metal Rat, page 41)

Stir-Fried Octopus (*Nakji Bokkeumbap*) – (See Water Dog, page 162)

Fried Rice (*Bokkeumbap*) – (See Water Dog, page 161)

Sautéed Zucchini and Loofah (*Hobak Namul*) (See Wood Monkey, page 142)

Fruit Medley (See Earth Rat, page 49)

Assorted Rice Cakes

Winter

TONG-JI OR WINTER SOLSTICE DAY

Tong-ji is the shortest day of the year, occurring December 21 or 22. This holiday began as a tactic to chase away the blues when daylight was the scarcest. Red Bean Porridge with Rice Balls was the traditional food for this day. Children would eat as many rice balls as their age. Nowadays, families still use the occasion to gather close together.

Nothing creates a cozier feeling on a long winter night than huddling around a hot pot! Even better, it's the easiest Korean meal to make—almost no preparation or clean up. Using chopsticks or long fondue forks, everyone simmers their own meat, vegetables, shellfish, or tofu in the bubbling broth. It's the forerunner of the one-dish meal. Traditionally, a Korean fire pot or charcoal brazier was used for cooking at the table. Small slivers of charred wood fueled the flame in the central cylinder, while sparks shot out the top of the fire pot. A modern day counterpart (and safer method) is the electric fondue pot.

Place the fondue pot in the center of the table, with everyone seated around it. Surround the pot with platters of very thinly sliced meat, bite-sized vegetables, shellfish, very firm tofu, and sauces. Arrange chopsticks or long fondue forks at each place setting, so everyone can cook their own dinner, piece by piece. Dab spoonfuls of the sauces onto each plate, so everyone can dip the tidbits. It's a great way to spend a cold wintry evening, talking and laughing around the steaming hot pot. All you have to do is keep the broth bubbling! The rest takes care of itself.

Korean Hot Pot

Korean Hot Pot (*Shinsollo*) – (See Fire Rat, page 46)

Buckwheat Noodles (*Mul Naeng Myun*) – (See Wood Ox, page 58)

Cellophane Noodles (*Dang Myun*) – (See Wood Sheep, page 132)

Seasoned Dipping Sauce (*Yang Yeum Kanjang*) – (See Fire Rat, page 47)

Sweet and Sour Dipping Sauce (*Tong Su Boekum*) – (See Fire Rat, page 47)

Sweet Anchovy Condiment (*Marun Panchan*) – (See Earth Rooster, page 157)

Tangerines

Roasted Chestnuts

Dried Persimmons

PAEGIL: HUNDREDTH DAY

Paegil or *Baek-il* is the celebration of a baby surviving its first hundred days of life. In times past, the mortality rate for infants was high. If the child lived through the first hundred days, the odds were that it would survive into adulthood, and the grateful parents held a party as a reaffirmation of life.

Today the custom continues as a charming rite of passage. The proud parents have their baby photographed at a studio and, not unexpectedly, have a party. To announce their baby's Hundredth Day party, they send rice cakes to relatives and close friends. In turn, the guests arrive with gifts of money, symbolizing wealth for the baby, or items made with thread or yarn, representing their wishes for the baby's long life.

TOL: FIRST BIRTHDAY

Tol is a more significant feast held on the baby's first birthday. The child is outfitted in traditional Korean dress. The focus of this celebration is a custom where the baby predicts his or her own future. A number of objects is arranged on a table. Tradition holds that the first object the child picks up will foretell his or her career. A writing brush or book means the baby will be a scholar. Money or rice predicts wealth. An arrow or dagger suggests a military career. The choice of thread means long life. The guests contribute to the occasion with gifts of clothing, money, or gold jewelry for the birthday baby. What better way to strengthen family ties than to welcome the newest family member with good times and good food?

Family Reunion – Dinner for Eight

Oxtail Soup (*Sokkori gom tang*) – (See Water Monkey, page 139)

Water Kimchi (*Na Bak Kimchi*) – (See Fire Monkey, page 143)

Pork and Cabbage Pinwheels – (See Wood Monkey, page 140)

Layered Beef and Cabbage Pie – (See Wood Boar, page 174)

Sweet and Sour Tofu (*Tong Su Tubu*) – (See Wood Rooster, page 154)

Steamed Rice (*Bap*) – (See Earth Dragon, page 106)

Sautéed Oriental Eggplant (*Gaji Namul*) – (See Fire Dragon, page 105)

Crispy Lotus Root – (See Metal Dog, page 159)

Red Peppers and Potatoes (*Gam za chorim*) – (See Metal Monkey, page 137)

Cream of Pine Nut Bisque (*Jat Juk*) – (See Earth Dog, page 167)

Assorted Rice Cakes

ENTERTAINING

KOREAN DINNER ETIQUETTE

Traditional Korean tables are set in a specific manner with certain rules. The table setting consists of three rows. In the first row, the rice is placed to the left. Soup is placed to the right, with an extra dish beside it for discardable items such as shells or bones. A spoon and chopsticks are placed to the right.

It is worth noting that, unlike most Asians, Koreans eat rice with a large spoon, reserving chopsticks for side dishes and entrées. Utensils should be metal, even silver, but not wood, bamboo, or plastic.

The second row consists of kimchi in the center, with soy sauce and other condiments placed beside it, and water or barley tea placed on the right. The third row, made up of dishes that can be eaten with a spoon, such as stews and soups, is placed on the right. Side dishes, entrées, or any food that is eaten with chopsticks is placed on the left.

DINING DOS AND DON'TS

Meals epitomize the communal nature of Korea. If main dishes or even side dishes, called *banchan*, are placed in the middle of the table, it means that they are to be shared, family style. Communal eating is the norm, so several rules of etiquette need to be observed.

Dos

- Do wish your hosts or dinner partners, *jal mok kessum nida*, the Korean counterpart of *bon appetit*.
- Do spoon rice into your own soup bowl, not the communal tureen.
- Do ask for more *banchan*, but only when the first bowl is empty.
- Do pour tea or beer for friends when the cups are empty.
- Do eat rice with a spoon.
- Do use the proper dipping sauce for each food. If unsure which sauce belongs with which food, ask.

Don'ts

- Don't spike the spoon or chopsticks into rice. This act is performed during ancestor worship, indicating that the rice is reserved for the deceased. It is considered very rude at any other occasion.
- Don't punctuate a point by waving the chopsticks in the air.
- Don't hoard food. Take only a morsel or two. Be sure that everyone has a chance to sample each dish before taking more.
- Don't "fish around" in communal dishes with your spoon or chopsticks. Only touch food that you are going to eat. If a morsel is touched by accident, remove it to your plate.
- Don't return uneaten or partially eaten food to communal dishes.
- Don't blow your nose at the table.
- Don't eat until the eldest person begins the meal.

KOREAN DRINKING ETIQUETTE

Koreans rarely drink anything alcoholic with their meals. The only beverages are water or barley tea. However, when they do imbibe, Koreans drink a wide variety of beverages. Teahouses and coffee shops abound. Besides beer, Korea has many different types of traditional alcoholic drinks. *Soju* is the most popular, while other common drinks include *makkoli* and *dong-dong-ju* (white-colored drinks fermented from rice).

Several rules apply to drinking in the Korean culture.
- The most important is the two-hand rule. This requires that you use both hands to pour or accept a drink. Both hands should be used to make a toast. Exceptions where the two-hand rule does not apply would be to friends of the same age, or a father pouring *soju* into his son's glass. Both hands on the bottle, or one hand on the bottle and the other on the forearm, shows respect for the person whose drink you are pouring.
- Never pour your own drink unless it's from your own beer bottle. Your host, guest, or drinking buddy will pour your shot.
- If an acquaintance taps one of your two hands over drinks, it indicates he wants to become friends.
- When someone pours you a drink, immediately reciprocate. If the other person's glass is not empty, it is common to ask them to finish the drink (bottoms up!) before refilling their glass.
- With few exceptions, women do not pour drinks for men. Korean women do not wish to be mentally associated with the bar hostess profession.
- "Cheers" in Korean is *"geonbae."* No eloquent speech is necessary before toasting. In fact, Koreans like to accentuate something brought up during conversation by raising a toast to it. A common expression is *"keureon euimi ro,"* which roughly translates to, "on that note, cheers!"

WINTER

Rat

Metal Rat

January 31,1900 — February 18, 1901
January 28, 1960 — February 14, 1961

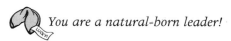 *You are a natural-born leader!*

Auspicious Foods
Bean soup, peaches, spicy flavors.

Grilled Pollack and Scallions

BUGO KOCHUCHANG GUI

> *1 pound pollack, cod, or other fish fillets*
> *2 tablespoons soy paste (available in Asian supermarkets)*
> *1 tablespoon red pepper powder, or to taste (available in*
> *   Asian supermarkets)*
> *1 tablespoon soy sauce*
> *1 tablespoon molasses*
> *1 tablespoon rice wine*
> *1 tablespoon sesame oil*
> *½ tablespoon sesame seeds*
> *4 tablespoons minced scallions*
> *2 tablespoons minced garlic*
> *2 tablespoons minced fresh ginger*

If necessary, thaw the fish and rinse under running water. Separate
or cut into 4 portions. Place the 4 fillets on squares of aluminum
foil that are large enough to fold into pouches.

Combine the remaining ingredients with 2 tablespoons water. Divide equally among the 4 fillets and spoon over the tops. Wrap the foil around each portion to create packets.

Place on a hot grill and roast for 8 to 10 minutes, or until the fish flakes easily with a fork. When the packets are cool enough to handle, remove the fish from the foil.

Caution: Be careful of the hot steam escaping from the foil pouches!

YIELDS 4 SERVINGS OR 8 APPETIZERS.

Alternative: Instead of 4 portions of pollack, cut the fish into 8 pieces. Prepare as above, but wrap in 8 foil packets to create 8 appetizers.

Alternative: Instead of placing the foil packets on the grill, pop them into a pre-heated 350°F oven for 12 to 14 minutes, or until the fish flakes easily with a fork.

Water Rat

February 18, 1912 – February 5, 1913
February 15, 1972 – February 2, 1973

 *You are a perfectionist and a humanitarian.*

Auspicious Foods
Bean soup, chestnuts, salty flavors.

Taro Soup

KUK

1 ½ pounds taro roots
2 ounces shrimp
1 tablespoon soy sauce, or to taste
1 green onion, finely sliced
1 teaspoon salt, or to taste
1 tablespoon sesame oil
¼ cup chopped cilantro
4 cilantro sprigs

Peel and cut the taro into ½-inch cubes. Peel, clean, and dice the shrimp. Marinate the shrimp with the soy sauce and green onion. Bring 1 quart water and the salt to a boil. Lower the heat. Add the shrimp mixture and taro. Cook over medium heat for 20 to 22 minutes, or until the taro is tender. Stir in the oil and chopped cilantro. Serve hot, garnished with cilantro sprigs.

YIELDS 4 SERVINGS.

Garlic Beef Roll-ups

½ pound beef
24 cloves garlic
2 tablespoons finely sliced ginger
4 tablespoons julienned green onion
2 tablespoons soy sauce
2 tablespoons rice wine
2 tablespoons molasses
⅛ teaspoon ground black pepper, or to taste
2 tablespoons sesame oil
2 teaspoons sesame seeds

Slice the beef paper-thin into ½ by 2-inch strips. Place a garlic clove at one end of a beef strip. Roll up and secure with a toothpick. Continue until all the garlic cloves and beef strips are used.

Place ½ cup water in a large skillet. Add the beef roll-ups, ginger, green onion, soy sauce, rice wine, molasses, and pepper. Bring to a boil, lower the heat, cover, and allow to steam for 10 to 12 minutes, or until the beef is tender and the juices have been absorbed. Stir occasionally to cook evenly. Add a tablespoon of water, if necessary. Remove from heat and drizzle with the sesame oil, turning with a spoon or tongs to coat the roll-ups evenly.

If serving as appetizers, garnish with sesame seeds and arrange on a heated platter. If serving as a side dish, remove the toothpicks when the roll-ups are cool enough to handle. Garnish with the sesame seeds and serve.

YIELDS 2 DOZEN APPETIZERS OR 4 SERVINGS.

Wood Rat

February 5, 1924 – January 23, 1925
February 2, 1984 – February 19, 1985

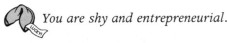 *You are shy and entrepreneurial.*

Auspicious Foods
Bean soup, heart of palm, sour flavors.

Pickled Napa Cabbage

Pom Kimchi

2 pounds napa cabbage
¼ cup rock salt
1 tablespoon crushed garlic
1 tablespoon grated fresh ginger
2 green onions, minced
1 tablespoon raw sugar or light brown sugar
1 tablespoon soy sauce
1 tablespoon ground red pepper
2 tablespoons minced dried shrimp

Rinse the cabbage and drain well. Slice into 1-inch pieces. Place in a large mixing bowl. Sprinkle with salt. Mix well, kneading with hands, and press down. Set aside for 5 hours, turning and kneading cabbage once an hour. Squeeze the cabbage and drain thoroughly.

Mix all the remaining ingredients. Fold into the cabbage, kneading it with your hands to evenly distribute the spices. Place in a clean crock or large jar with a tight fitting lid. Serve immediately or keep in the refrigerator for up to 2 weeks.

YIELDS 2 POUNDS.

Hint: Flavor improves with age.

Fire Rat

January 24, 1936 – February 10, 1937
February 19, 1996 – February 6, 1997

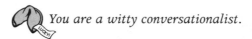 *You are a witty conversationalist.*

Auspicious Foods
Bean soup, almonds, bitter flavors.

Korean Hot Pot

SHINSOLLO

Traditionally the meat is sliced while frozen, the result being extremely thin circles of beef or lamb, which are rolled into easily managed pieces for skewering and simmering.

2 quarts vegetable or beef broth
1 pound sea scallops or shrimp, cleaned and shelled
½ pound beef or lamb, very thinly sliced
½ pound firm tofu, cubed
1 small head (about 1 pound) cabbage, broken into leaves
2 cups straw mushrooms (available in Asian supermarkets)
 or 2 cups sliced button mushrooms
2 cups mung bean sprouts
8 baby bok choy, optional (available in Asian supermarkets)
2 cups cooked buckwheat noodles (available in Asian super-
 markets) or 2 cups cooked rice noodles

Heat the broth in a 3-quart pot. Carefully transfer the broth to the hot pot or fondue pot, or bring the broth to a boil in the hot pot or fondue pot. (Be careful—remember this is *boiling hot!*) Using chopsticks or long forks, fondue style, dip a piece of shellfish, meat, tofu, or vegetable in the boiling broth, and simmer until it is cooked. Next dip it in sauce (recipes follow), cool, and eat. Serve with noodles.

YIELDS **8** SERVINGS.

Seasoned Dipping Sauce

Yang Yeum Kanjang

Ko chu garu is dried and powdered red peppers. If coarsely ground, this fiery spice is used for making kimchi. If finely ground, it is used in sauces. Either way, it adds pizzazz to any dish!

½ cup soy sauce
½ tablespoon toasted sesame seeds, crushed in a mortar
1 tablespoon sesame oil
1 tablespoon rice vinegar
1 tablespoon thinly sliced green onion
¼ teaspoon hot red chili powder (available in Asian super-markets), or to taste
1 teaspoon sugar
⅛ teaspoon white pepper

Combine all the ingredients and mix thoroughly. The sauce may be stored in the refrigerator for up to 1 week.

YIELDS 1 CUP.

Sweet and Sour Dipping Sauce

Tong Su Boekum

¼ cup rice vinegar
¼ cup sugar
¼ cup fish sauce (available in Asian supermarkets)
1 tablespoon shredded carrots
¼ teaspoon chopped red chilies
1 clove garlic, minced

Combine the vinegar, 1 tablespoon water, sugar, and fish sauce. Fold in the carrot, chilies, and garlic. Mix well and set aside. Allow the flavors to blend for at least 2 hours before serving.

YIELDS 1 CUP.

Earth Rat

February 10, 1948 – January 28, 1949

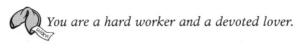 *You are a hard worker and a devoted lover.*

Auspicious Foods
Bean soup, dates, sweet flavors.

Barley Water Tea

Bori Cha

Tea is not the venerated elixir in Korea that it is in China. Barley water tea is considered a digestive aid when sipped after dinner. This pale, delicately flavored tea may be served hot or cold.

2 tablespoons unhulled barley
4 $\frac{1}{4}$ cups boiling water

Brown the barley in a large pan over low heat for 10 to 12 minutes, shaking often, until the toasted grains are a dark brown.

Place the barley grains into the boiling water. Simmer for 18 to 20 minutes. Strain and serve hot or refrigerate and serve cold.

Yields 4 servings.

Fruit Medley

1 pineapple
1 large honeydew melon
1 papaya, peeled, seeded, and cut into chunks
3 tangerines, peeled and sectioned
4 kiwis, peeled, sliced, and cut in half
2 peaches, pitted, peeled, and cut into chunks
2 tablespoons lime juice

Slice the pineapple lengthwise and discard the core. Reserving the "shells," cut pineapple into bite-sized chunks. Using a zigzag motion, cut the honeydew melon in a saw-tooth pattern. Reserving the "shells," seed and cut the honeydew into chunks. Combine all the fruit chunks and lime juice, tossing lightly, just until the lime juice evenly coats each morsel. Heap the fruit high in the hollowed-out pineapple and honeydew halves.

YIELDS **8** SERVINGS.

Ox

BETWEEN SEASONS

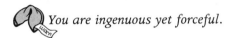

Metal Ox

February 19, 1901 to February 7, 1902
February 15, 1961 to February 4, 1962

You are ingenuous yet forceful.

Auspicious Foods
Tofu, bird's nest soup, peaches, spicy flavors.

Lettuce Wraps

SANGCHU SSAM

Lettuce Wraps are Korean-style tacos, eaten out-of-hand. Traditionally, fresh sesame leaves are used. The leaves lend a delightfully distinctive flavor, similar to that of basil, but if sesame leaves are unavailable, use whole Bibb lettuce leaves or cut iceberg leaves.

This is an ideal dish to use up leftover beef, chicken, or rice.

½ pound Barbecued Beef (see recipe page 98)
2 cups cooked rice
½ cup julienned carrots
½ cup coarsely chopped water chestnuts, optional
1 teaspoon toasted sesame seeds
12 sesame leaves (available in Asian supermarkets)
*   or 1 head Bibb or iceberg lettuce*
Sesame Soy Dip (see following recipe)

Coarsely chop the barbecued beef. Combine it thoroughly with the rice, carrots, water chestnuts, and sesame seeds. Refrigerate and allow flavors to marry for at least 30 minutes.

To trim the lettuce leaves, arrange the rinsed and dried leaves on a clean cutting surface. Place a bowl on top of the leaves and trim around the bowl, cutting off the edges and leaving the crisp, central portion of the leaves. Reserve the lettuce trimmings for a salad.

Serve the lettuce and the beef mixture separately. Let people help themselves, spooning the beef mixture into a lettuce leaf and rolling it up like a taco. Top with Sesame Soy Dip.

YIELDS 4 APPETIZER SERVINGS OR 2 ENTRÉE SERVINGS.

Sesame Soy Dip

SSAM JANG

1 clove garlic, minced
2 tablespoons ground beef
1 tablespoon sesame oil
½ teaspoon chili pepper, or to taste
3 tablespoons soybean paste (available in Asian super-
   markets)
1 green onion, finely sliced

Sauté the garlic and beef in the oil. Stir in the pepper and soybean paste. Add 2 tablespoons water. Heat through, stirring continuously. Remove from the heat and add the green onion.

YIELDS ¾ CUP.

Water Ox

February 6, 1913 to January 25, 1914
February 3, 1973 to January 22, 1974

 *You are self-assured and open-minded.*

Auspicious Foods
Tofu, bird's nest soup, chestnuts, salty flavors.

Cornish Hen Soup with Chestnuts

YONG KEH BAIKSUK

In the past, hens were considered a rare luxury, reserved only for special occasions. Even today, this treat is sure to surprise and delight the palate. Nowadays, this soup is a favorite hot-weather meal. Whether or not you believe in the medicinal properties of ginseng, this is a dish your guests will enjoy!

Serve each person a bowl of soup containing a whole hen. Accompany each bowl with an individual salter (small condiment dish,) containing a salt, black pepper, and sesame seed mixture for dipping.

> *1 cup sweet rice (available in Asian supermarkets)*
> *18 cloves garlic*
> *18 chestnuts, cooked and shelled*
> *18 jujubes (Korean red pitted dates; available in Asian*
> * supermarkets)*
> *6 Cornish hens*
> *1 tablespoon sliced fresh ginger*
> *6 (1-inch) pieces fresh ginseng, optional*
> *3 tablespoons salt*
> *¹/₂ teaspoon ground black pepper*
> *2 tablespoons sesame seeds*
> *3 green onions, diagonally sliced*

Cover the rice with water and allow to soak overnight. Drain. Combine the rice with the peeled garlic, chestnuts, and jujubes. Rinse the hens and pat dry. Stuff the cavities of the hens with the mixture and stitch the cavity with thread, being sure to completely sew it shut.

To 2 quarts of boiling water, add the ginger, ginseng, hens, and 1 tablespoon salt. Simmer for 1 hour or until the hens are thoroughly cooked. Remove the hens from the broth and pull out the cavities' threads.

Combine the remaining 2 tablespoons salt with the black pepper and sesame seeds. Distribute evenly among 6 salters or tiny condiment dishes.

Place each hen, breast-side up, in a large bowl. Ladle hot broth over it, and garnish with green onion slivers. Present each guest a bowl of soup and a condiment dish.

YIELDS 6 SERVINGS.

Hint: Recipe may be doubled.

Capon with Ginseng and Korean Dates

The young chicken is cooked in a traditional *tukbaege*, or pot, with ginseng and jujubes and then brought still bubbling to the table. The ginseng, or *insam*, is prepared and eaten like a vegetable, although it is said to have rejuvenating properties. Its flavor has been described as that of parsnip and ginger, a subtle flavor with a bite. The jujubes are dried Korean dates that lend a sweet contrast to the soup. Serve the stew in a *tukbaege* or tureen, letting guests help themselves to the tender capon, rice, and rich broth.

This dish lends itself perfectly to the Korean custom of eating rice and soup with a spoon. Only meat and side dishes are eaten with chopsticks.

> *2 small (about 1 pound each) capons*
> * or 4 Cornish hens*
> *4 pieces (½ by 1-inch long) fresh ginseng*
> *1 cup sticky rice; well rinsed*
> *4 green onions, thinly sliced*
> *12 pitted jujubes (dried Korean dates)*
> *4 cloves garlic, sliced*
> *¼ cup sesame seeds, toasted*
> *1 tablespoon sesame oil*
> *¼ teaspoon ground black pepper*

Rinse the capons and pat dry. Scrape off the ginseng peel. Combine the ginseng, rice, green onions, 6 jujubes, and 2 garlic cloves. Stuff the capons, and tie shut the openings with small skewers.

Place the capons in a *tukbaege* or a 2-quart covered pot. Add 1 quart water, the remaining 6 jujubes and 2 garlic cloves, the sesame seeds, sesame oil, and pepper. Bring to a boil, cover the pot, and reduce heat.

Simmer for 1 hour, or until the capons are tender and the meat is pulling away from the bones. Very carefully remove the skewers from the capons. Serve piping hot in the *tukbaege* or a pre-warmed tureen.

YIELDS 4 SERVINGS.

Wood Ox

January 25, 1925 to February 12, 1926
February 20, 1985 to February 8, 1986

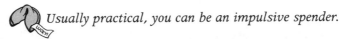 *Usually practical, you can be an impulsive spender.*

Auspicious Foods
Tofu, bird's nest soup, heart of palm, sour flavors.

Buckwheat Noodles

MUL NAENG MYUN

Buckwheat noodles are served chilled during the summer because of their refreshing appeal. Present the chewy noodles in frosty bowls that have been chilled in the freezer for an hour. Serve with rice wine vinegar and hot mustard. Let the guests season their noodles to suit their own tastes.

> *3 tablespoons raw sugar or light brown sugar*
> *3 tablespoons rice wine vinegar*
> *1 teaspoon soy sauce*
> *1 tablespoon salt*
> *1 cup julienned cooked beef*
> *4 green onions, thinly sliced*
> *¼ teaspoon ground black pepper*
> *1 teaspoon toasted sesame seeds*
> *6 cups beef bouillon*
> *1 cup coarsely chopped Asian pear (available in Asian supermarkets)*
> *½ cup coarsely chopped daikon (available in Asian supermarkets) or cucumber*
> *1 pound buckwheat noodles (available in Asian supermarkets)*
> *1 tablespoon sesame oil*

Add 1 tablespoon of the sugar, 1 tablespoon of the vinegar, the soy sauce, 1 teaspoon of the salt, the beef, green onions, black pepper, and sesame seeds to the bouillon. Stir and refrigerate for at least an hour.

Combine the remaining 2 tablespoons sugar, 2 tablespoons vinegar, and 1 teaspoon salt with the pear and daikon. Allow flavors to marry for at least 30 minutes.

Stir the remaining 1 teaspoon salt into 2 quarts boiling water. Add the noodles and follow the package directions, cooking for 8 to 10 minutes, or until the noodles are tender-crisp. Rinse in cold water. Mix gently with the sesame oil and refrigerate for at least 30 minutes.

Combine the bouillon, pear mixture, and noodles. Ladle into icy bowls and serve with a shaker of rice wine vinegar and individual condiment dishes of hot mustard.

YIELDS 4 SERVINGS.

Hint: On wintry days, serve the noodles hot in steaming broth.

Fire Ox

February 11, 1937 to January 30, 1938
February 7, 1997 to January 27, 1998

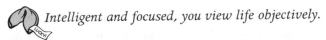 *Intelligent and focused, you view life objectively.*

Auspicious Foods
Tofu, bird's nest soup, almonds, bitter flavors.

Sticky Rice

BAP

1 ½ cups sticky rice (available in Asian supermarkets)

Using a colander or sieve, rinse the rice under running water until clear. Cover the rice with water to a height of about 1 inch above the rice. Soak overnight and drain.

If using a rice cooker, follow manufacturer's directions. If making rice the traditional way, use a steamer. Fill the lower half with water and bring it to a boil. Fill the upper half with the drained rice, taking care that the bottom of the basket does not touch the water. Cover, lower the heat to a simmer, and steam the rice for 25 to 30 minutes, or until the rice looks glossy and translucent. If the rice is still undercooked, cover and steam another 4 to 5 minutes. It is better to overcook a little rather than undercook this type of rice.

YIELDS 3 ½ CUPS.

Earth Ox

January 29, 1949 to February 16, 1950

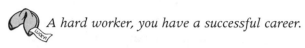 *A hard worker, you have a successful career.*

Auspicious Foods
Tofu, bird's nest soup, dates, sweet flavors.

Azalea Pancakes

JINDALAE HWAJUN

> *3 cups glutinous rice powder (available in Asian*
> *supermarkets)*
> *½ teaspoon salt*
> *30 azalea petals*
> *2 ounces mugwort leaves (available in Asian supermarkets)*
> *3 tablespoons peanut oil*
> *¼ cup honey or light brown sugar*
> *1 teaspoon cinnamon*
> *½ cup crushed pine nuts*

Add 1 ¼ cups boiling water and salt to the glutinous rice powder. Mix thoroughly. When cool enough to handle, knead the dough. Roll to a ½-inch thickness.

Rinse the azalea flowers carefully, pat dry, and remove stamens and pistils. Rinse the mugwort leaves, using only the leaves' tender tips. Pat dry. Arrange the petals and leaves on the dough, pressing them lightly to set them. Centering the floral arrangements on the pancakes, use a small glass or cookie cutter to cut them into 2-inch rounds.

Add oil to a skillet or griddle and pan-fry the cakes, cooking for 1 minute on each side, or until golden brown. Carefully remove with a spatula. Drizzle with honey or sprinkle with sugar. Dust lightly with cinnamon and pine nuts.

YIELDS 30 PANCAKES.

Chrysanthemum Pancakes: In the autumn, use chrysanthemum petals instead of azaleas. Celebrate the fall season by adorning the hwajun with golden mum petals that replicate the flower's image.

Azalea Punch

JINDALAE HWACHAE

1 cup omija *(fruit of* Maximowiczia typical; *available in Asian supermarkets)*
1 cup raw sugar or light brown sugar
1 cup honey
20 azalea flowers
2 tablespoons mung-bean starch
1 teaspoon pine nuts

Gently wash the omija and place in a ceramic or glass bowl. (Metal pots interact chemically and change the color of the fruit.) Cover with 2 quarts warm water and set aside overnight, or for a minimum of 6 hours. Strain the omija water through clean muslin. Add the sugar and honey to the omija water. Chill and set aside.

Rinse the azalea flowers carefully, pat dry, and remove stamens and pistils. Dust the flowers with mung-bean starch and briefly blanch in boiling water. Gently rinse in cold water and pat dry.

To serve, place the flowers in a bowl and cover with the chilled omija water. Garnish with pine nuts.

YIELDS 2 QUARTS.

Tiger

SPRING

Metal Tiger

February 17, 1950 to February 5, 1951

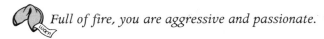 *Full of fire, you are aggressive and passionate.*

Auspicious Foods
Hearty soup, oolong tea, peaches, spicy flavors.

Korean Rice Breakfast

KONGNAMUL KUK BAP

Traditionally 4 side dishes are served with this breakfast: cabbage kimchi, radish kimchi, salted baby shrimp, and shredded beef in soy sauce.

1 ½ cups bean sprouts
4 ½ cups cooked rice
1 ½ teaspoons salt
6 eggs
6 teaspoons toasted sesame seeds
4 to 6 teaspoons hot red chili powder, or to taste
6 green onions, thinly sliced
1 teaspoon pepper, or to taste

Blanch the bean sprouts in 2 cups boiling water for 5 minutes. Drain, reserving liquid. Add enough hot water to make 6 cups. Put back in pot and add the rice, bean sprouts, and salt. Break the eggs into the pot. Sprinkle with the sesame seeds, chili powder, green onions, and pepper.

Cover and cook over moderate heat until it comes to a boil. Do not stir. Cook for 2 to 3 minutes, or until the eggs begin to set. Remove the mixture from the heat. Break the egg yolks and blend all into a congee. Serve hot in individual bowls.

YIELDS 6 SERVINGS.

Persimmon Punch

SUJONGGWA

12 dried persimmons
½ cup pine nuts
¼ pound ginger
2 cinnamon sticks
2 cups raw sugar or brown sugar

Remove the seeds from the dried persimmons. Replace each seed with 6 pine nuts.

Scrape the ginger and slice thinly; it should make about ½ cup. Simmer the ginger and cinnamon sticks in 1 gallon water for ½ hour. (Breathe the aroma!) Stir in the sugar and bring to a boil. Add the persimmons, stirring gently. Turn off the heat and let cool.

When the mixture has cooled, pour into a large, covered container. Refrigerate overnight, allowing the persimmons to plump up. The punch becomes a pale rose color. Strain the spicy punch before serving. Garnish with remaining pine nuts. (Reserve the persimmons for a delectable dessert.)

YIELDS 1 GALLON.

Water Tiger

February 8, 1902 to January 28, 1903
February 5, 1962 to January 24, 1963

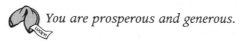 *You are prosperous and generous.*

Auspicious Foods
Hearty soup, oolong tea, chestnuts, salty flavors.

Nine-section Dish

KUJULPAN

This is an elegant hors d'oeuvre platter for very special occasions. This selection of appetizing ingredients is served in an octagonal dish with a central, ninth compartment for miniature Korean pancakes. The other eight compartments hold various meat or vegetable fillings. Each person selects the fillings, wraps them up in a pancake, and eats the concoction out of hand like a taco.

Hint. Double the recipe and make a meal for four.

> *½ pound shrimp, cooked and shelled*
> *1 ¼ teaspoons salt, plus additional to taste*
> *1 tablespoon plus 2 teaspoons sugar*
> *¼ cup rice vinegar*
> *¼ pound cooked beef*
> *2 teaspoons light soy sauce*
> *1 tablespoon minced green onion*
> *2 cloves garlic, crushed*
> *6 tablespoons sesame oil*
> *1 medium cucumber*
> *1 medium carrot*
> *½ cup sliced shiitake mushrooms*
> *2 eggs, beaten*

*4 ounces bellflower roots (*Campanula takesimana*)*
or 1 small daikon (white radish)
4 ounces bamboo shoots
8 (3-inch) pancakes (recipe follows)

Clean and slice the shrimp into thin strips. Mix with ½ teaspoon salt, 1 tablespoon sugar, and the vinegar. Allow shrimp to marinate for at least 1 hour.

Slice the beef into thin strips. Mix with 1 teaspoon soy sauce, the green onion, and 1 crushed garlic clove. Stir-fry in 1 tablespoon oil for 2 to 3 minutes, or until heated through. Set aside and keep warm.

Peel the cucumber and carrot. Slice into ¼ by 2-inch slices (about 1 cup each). Sprinkle with ¼ teaspoon salt. Squeeze out the excess water. Stir-fry in 1 tablespoon oil for 3 to 4 minutes, or until tender-crisp. Set aside and keep warm.

Gently toss the mushrooms with 1 teaspoon soy sauce and 1 teaspoon sugar. Stir-fry in 1 tablespoon oil 1 to 2 minutes, or until tender-crisp. Set aside and keep warm.

Add salt to taste to the beaten eggs and stir-fry in 1 tablespoon oil 1 to 2 minutes, or until the eggs have set. When cool enough to handle, slice the scrambled eggs into ½ by 1-inch pieces. Set aside and keep warm.

Blanch the bellflower roots. Peel and shred the bellflower roots or daikon (about ¼ cup). Add in ½ teaspoon salt and remaining 1 clove garlic. Stir-fry in 1 tablespoon oil. Set aside and keep warm.

Slice the bamboo into thin, 1-inch strips. Sprinkle with 1 teaspoon sugar and stir-fry in 1 tablespoon oil for 2 to 3 minutes, or until tender-crisp.

Arrange each of the fillings in one of the 8 compartments. (The beef will fill 2 compartments.) Place the pancakes in the central compartment and serve.

YIELDS 4 SERVINGS.

Korean Pancakes

2 eggs, beaten
½ cup plus 1 tablespoon milk
½ cup sifted all-purpose flour
2 teaspoons sugar
¼ teaspoon salt
1 tablespoon sesame oil

Combine the eggs and milk. Sift the flour, sugar, and salt. Fold the dry ingredients into the egg mixture, mixing until smooth.

Drop batter by tablespoon onto a hot, oiled pan or griddle. Spread batter evenly for thin pancakes. When underside is golden brown, flip with spatula. Remove when both sides are done.

YIELDS 8 (3-INCH) PANCAKES.

Mung Bean Pancakes

PINDAETTOK

2 cups shelled dried mung beans
4 cloves garlic, crushed
3 tablespoons peanut oil
1 tablespoon minced ginger
1/2 pound boneless loin of pork, julienned
1/2 teaspoon salt, or to taste
1 cup chopped leek (white part only) or chopped onion
1/2 cup green beans (fresh or frozen), chopped small
1/4 cup soy sauce

Soak the mung beans in hot tap water overnight.

Heat a wok or frying pan and stir-fry 1 clove garlic in 2 tablespoons peanut oil. Add 1 teaspoon ginger, the pork, and 1/2 teaspoon salt. Stir-fry 10 minutes or until the pork is thoroughly cooked. Add the leek and green beans. Stir-fry 5 minutes, or tender-crisp. Set aside to cool.

Drain the mung beans, place in a food processor, and pulse chop. Add 1 1/2 cups water, the soy sauce, and the remaining 3 cloves garlic and 2 teaspoons ginger. Puree until smooth. Add the pork mixture. Let the batter stand for 30 minutes.

Drizzle some of the remaining 1 tablespoon oil in a 9-inch skillet. Making 1 pancake at a time, pour 2/3 cup batter into the skillet and fry for 1 minute each side, turning once, until golden brown. Keep cooked pancakes warm. Repeat the process for each pancake.

YIELDS 6 PANCAKES.

Wood Tiger

January 26, 1914 to February 13, 1915
January 23, 1974 to February 10, 1975

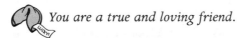 *You are a true and loving friend.*

Auspicious Foods
Hearty soup, oolong tea, heart of palm, sour flavors.

Pickled White Radish

YUL MU KIMCHI

1 pound daikon (white radish)
2 teaspoons salt
2 teaspoons sugar
1 whole jalapeño pepper or 2 teaspoons chili powder,
* or to taste*

Peel the daikon and cut into 2 by ½-inch strips (4 cups). Combine all ingredients in a clean glass or pottery container. Cover. Store at room temperature for 2 days to ferment. Serve and refrigerate any remaining pickled radish.

YIELDS 4 CUPS.

Pickled Daikon

1 pound daikon (white radish)
12 cloves garlic, crushed
4 green onions, cut into 1-inch lengths
¼ cup chili powder, or to taste
2 tablespoons minced fresh ginger
½ teaspoon salt
1 teaspoon sugar
1 tablespoon brine shrimp, optional (available in Asian supermarkets)

Peel the daikon. Rinse and cut into 2 by ½-inch strips (4 cups). Combine all the ingredients in a clean glass or pottery container. Cover and store at room temperature for 24 hours to ferment. Refrigerate the remaining pickled daikon.

YIELDS 4 CUPS.

Sliced White Radish

Muu Namul

> 1 pound daikon (white radish; available in Asian super-
> markets)
> 1 tablespoon sesame oil
> 1 teaspoon roasted sesame seeds
> $\frac{1}{2}$ teaspoon salt, or to taste
> 2 cloves garlic, minced
> 1 teaspoon sugar
> $\frac{1}{8}$ teaspoon pepper, or to taste

Peel and slice the daikon into 3 by $\frac{1}{4}$-inch lengths (french-fry size).
Heat the oil in a skillet or wok and stir-fry the radish strips over
moderate heat for 1 to 2 minutes, or until softened. Sprinkle with
sesame seeds, salt, garlic, sugar, and pepper; mixing well. Serve at
room temperature as a vegetable side dish.

Yields 6 servings.

Fire Tiger

February 13, 1926 to February 1, 1927
February 9, 1986 to January 28, 1987

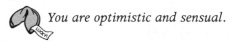 *You are optimistic and sensual.*

Auspicious Foods
Hearty soup, oolong tea, almonds, bitter flavors.

White Radish Soup

MU KUK

> 2 cups daikon (white radish; available in Asian supermarkets)
> 1 clove garlic, minced
> 1 teaspoon sesame oil
> $1/4$ cup soy sauce
> 1 small onion, sliced ($1/2$ cup)
> 8 cups beef broth
> $1/2$ pound chuck beef
> $1/8$ teaspoon ground black pepper
> $1/8$ teaspoon hot pepper seeds, optional
> 6 green onions, thinly sliced

Dice the daikon. Stir-fry the garlic in oil for 1 minute. Add the daikon, soy sauce, onion slices, and $1/2$ cup of the broth. Bring to a boil.

Trim and thinly slice the beef into 1-inch strips. Add the beef to the vegetables. Lower the heat, cover, and simmer for 15 minutes, or until the daikon is transparent.

Add the remaining 7 $1/2$ cups broth, bring the soup to a boil, then lower the heat and simmer for 15 minutes. Season with black pepper and pepper seeds. Sprinkle with green onions slices to garnish.

YIELDS 12 CUPS OR 6 LARGE BOWLS.

Stir-Fried Mugwort with Ginkgo Seeds

1 pound fresh mugwort leaves (available in Asian super-
markets)
2 teaspoons sesame oil
2 cloves garlic, minced
4 green onions, sliced
2 ounces (about ½ cup) ginkgo biloba seeds, boiled (avail-
able in Asian supermarkets)
1 teaspoon sesame seeds
¼ teaspoon salt, or to taste

Rinse and trim the mugwort leaves, using only the tender tips. Blanch the mugwort in 2 quarts boiling water for 1 minute. Remove the greens and drain thoroughly. Set aside.

In a hot wok or skillet, combine the oil, garlic, onions, and ginkgo biloba seeds. Stir-fry for 1 minute. Add the mugwort. Season with sesame seeds and salt. Stir-fry for 1 to 2 minutes, or until the flavors have married. Serve immediately.

YIELDS 4 SERVINGS.

Earth Tiger

January 31, 1938 to February 18, 1939
January 28, 1998 to February 15, 1999

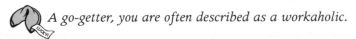 *A go-getter, you are often described as a workaholic.*

Auspicious Foods
Hearty soup, oolong tea, dates, sweet flavors.

Rice Cake Soup

TTOK KUK

Ttok Kuk is the traditional dish for New Year's Day. White rice cakes are customarily eaten because of an ancient belief that the first day of the new year should be somber and pure. Children make a game of eating the same number of rice cakes as their age.

½ pound beef brisket
2 cloves garlic
1 tablespoon instant beef or vegetable bouillon
1 (32-ounce) package Korean oval rice cakes (available in Asian supermarkets)
2 eggs, separated
2 tablespoons sesame oil
1 tablespoon soy sauce
1 teaspoon sesame seeds
1 teaspoon salt, or to taste
3 green onions, diagonally sliced

Bring 1 gallon water to boil in a large pot. Add the brisket, garlic, and bouillon. Reduce the heat and simmer for 3 hours or until the liquid reduces to two-thirds.

Soak the rice cakes in cold water for 1 hour. Remove the rice cakes.

The Best of Korean Cuisine

Scramble the yolks and whites of the eggs separately. Using 1 table-spoon of the sesame oil, fry the yolks into a thin omelet in a non-stick skillet over high heat, for 1 minute per side or until set. Fold or roll up the omelet and slice into thin strips. Repeat with the egg whites. Set aside.

Remove the brisket from pot but reserve the broth. Slice it into thin strips and combine with the soy sauce, sesame seeds, and remaining 1 tablespoon sesame oil. Increase the heat under the broth to high. When it comes to a rolling boil, add the rice cakes. Reduce the heat to medium and simmer the rice-cake ovals for 5 minutes, or until softened. Return the marinated beef to the soup. Salt to taste.

Ladle the steaming hot soup into large bowls. Garnish with sliced egg yolks, egg whites, and green-onion slivers.

YIELDS 6 SERVINGS.

Rice Cake and Dumpling Soup

Tтok Mandu Kuk

A modern counterpart to the Lunar New Year's traditional Rice Cake Soup is Rice Cake and Dumpling Soup, a heartier dish that, in addition to the customary oval rice cakes, includes *mandu*, Korean dumplings filled with spiced meats and vegetables.

Simply follow the recipe for Rice Cake Soup on page 76. Then make the dumplings. Estimate 3 to 4 dumplings per bowl. While piping hot, add the dumplings to the soup and serve immediately!

Spice Mixture
2 tablespoons chopped green onion
1 clove garlic, minced
2 tablespoons soy sauce
1 tablespoon minced ginger
1 tablespoon sesame oil
½ teaspoon salt, or to taste
¼ teaspoon ground black pepper

Combine all the ingredients.

Dumpling Filling
1 pound ground beef
4 cups mung bean sprouts
1 (8-ounce) package firm tofu
1 cup kimchi or shredded napa cabbage
1 cup finely chopped onion
1 tablespoon cornstarch
1 package (36 wrappers) wonton or gyoza wrappers
(available in Asian supermarkets) or make your own
wontons (see page 92)
1 tablespoon sesame oil
1 teaspoon salt

Thoroughly combine the beef and half the spice mixture. Set aside.

Blanch the bean sprouts in boiling water for 1 minute or until tender. Drain thoroughly. Drain the tofu and crumble into small bits. Chop the kimchi or cabbage and drain thoroughly. Combine the bean sprouts, tofu, kimchi, and onion with the remaining spice mixture. Be sure the spices are evenly distributed. Fold the vegetable mixture into the meat.

Whisk the cornstarch with 3 tablespoons cool water.

Take a wonton wrapper and lightly pat the surface with the cornstarch mixture. Place 1 teaspoon filling into the center of the wonton. Fold the wrapper in half and pinch or crimp the edges to seal it. Continue until all 36 wontons are complete. (Note: The wontons may be made the day before and refrigerated until the next step.)

Bring 2 quarts water to a boil. Add the oil and salt. Carefully add the dumplings with a slotted spoon. When the dumplings rise to the top, add 1 cup of cold water. Do not cover. Allow the water to come to a boil and the dumplings to rise to the top a second time. Carefully remove the dumplings with a slotted spoon, and add to the Rice Cake soup.

YIELDS 36 DUMPLINGS.

Alternative: Instead of beef, use pork, but be *sure* the meat is thoroughly cooked. Allow the dumplings to come to a boil 3 times instead of 2 by adding another cup of cold water after the second boil.

Alternative: Instead of adding the dumplings to soup, make a dumpling side dish. Serve with Vinegar Soy Sauce (recipe follows).

Vinegar Soy Sauce

This delectable sauce is perfect for dipping. Use with dumplings (page 78) or sweet and sour pork.

½ cup soy sauce
¼ cup rice wine vinegar or white vinegar
1 teaspoon raw sugar or light brown sugar
½ teaspoon sesame seeds
¼ teaspoon chili pepper seeds, optional

Combine all the ingredients. Allow to rest for 30 minutes for flavors to marry.

YIELDS 1 SCANT CUP.

Hint: Grind sesame seeds (*kkae so gum*) to better release their pungent flavor. Simply place the seeds in a rounded cup and crush them with the back of a teaspoon.

Sweet Rice

YAK BAP

1 ¾ cups short-grain rice
9 (1 cup) chestnuts, cooked, fresh or canned
6 red dates
¼ cup raisins
½ cup raw sugar or light brown sugar
1 tablespoon soy sauce
½ teaspoon cinnamon
4 teaspoons sesame oil
¼ cup pine nuts

Soak the rice in water for a minimum of 3 hours. Drain the rice.

Peel and quarter the chestnuts. Seed the dates. Combine the chestnuts, dates, raisins, sugar, soy sauce, and cinnamon. Allow flavors to marinate for an hour.

If using a rice cooker, pour 2 teaspoons sesame oil into a 5-cup rice cooker. Add the rice and 1 ½ cups water. Follow the rice cooker's directions.

If steaming the rice, bring the oil, rice, and water to a boil in a 2-quart pot. Lower the heat, cover, and simmer for 25 minutes, or until the moisture has been absorbed. Remove from the heat and allow to steam for 10 minutes.

When the rice is done, fold in the chestnut mixture. Add the pine nuts. Mix thoroughly. Spread the remaining 2 teaspoons sesame oil on a cookie sheet. Spread the rice mixture evenly and press to flatten. When the chewy dessert has cooled, cut with a wet knife.

YIELDS 1 DOZEN (1-INCH) SQUARES.

Rabbit

SPRING

Metal Rabbit

February 6, 1951 to January 26, 1952

*You are the star-maker, the brainpower
behind the successful person.*

Auspicious Foods
Spicy soup, noodles, peaches, spicy flavors.

Spicy Crab Soup

Doen Jang Jiege Keh

> *2 tablespoons* doen jang *bean paste (available in Asian
> supermarkets)*
> *2 cups soft tofu, cut in ½-inch cubes*
> *½ teaspoon red chili powder, or to taste*
> *1 tablespoon minced ginger*
> *1 teaspoon minced garlic*
> *½ cup sliced onion*
> *½ cup sliced zucchini*
> *1 pound cooked crab legs or 2 cooked crabs, each cut into 4
> pieces*

Combine 2 cups water and bean paste. Simmer in covered pot
over low flame for 8 to 10 minutes. Add tofu and simmer for 4 to
5 minutes. Add the chili powder, ginger, garlic, onion, zucchini,
and crab in shells. Steam for 12 to 15 minutes.

Yields 4 servings.

Grilled Spiced Fish

SEN SAEN YANG JUNG CHANG KUI

1 whole (1 ½ pounds) saltwater fish
  (flounder, red snapper, porgy, or mackerel)
1 teaspoon salt
2 cloves garlic, minced
1 teaspoon toasted sesame seeds
3 tablespoons sesame oil
2 tablespoons soy sauce
½ teaspoon chili pepper seeds, or to taste
⅛ teaspoon black pepper
4 green onions, slivered
1 stalk celery, slivered (½ cup)

Clean the fish. Remove the fins and gills. (Traditionally, Koreans grill the entire fish, including the head. This is optional.) Score the fish 6 times diagonally on each side. Rub the sides with salt and let stand for 15 minutes.

Combine the garlic, sesame seeds, oil, soy sauce, pepper seeds, pepper, and half the green onions. Mix and rub half the sauce onto the fish. Set aside for 15 minutes.

Using either a charcoal grill or a gas or electric broiler, grill fish for 6 minutes on each side. Remove and rub the balance of the marinade on the fish. Return to the broiler for 3 minutes, or until fish is tender.

Garnish with the remainder of the green onions and the slivered celery. Serve immediately on a heated platter.

YIELDS 6 SERVINGS.

Water Rabbit

January 29, 1903 to February 15, 1904
January 25, 1963 to February 12, 1964

 A loner, you must work at keeping relationships.

Auspicious Foods
Spicy soup, noodles, chestnuts, salty flavors.

Sesame Sauce

¼ cup light soy sauce
¼ cup dark soy sauce
¼ cup sesame oil
¼ cup sesame seeds
1 tablespoon sugar, or to taste
½ teaspoon freshly ground black pepper, or to taste

Combine all the ingredients.

YIELDS 1 CUP.

Bean-Thread Noodles

¼ cup (about 1 ounce) dried shiitake mushrooms
1 tablespoon (about ½ ounce) dried cloud ears
2 cups (about 7 ounces) uncooked bean-thread noodles
¼ cup peanut oil
1 carrot, peeled and grated
½ cup minced green pepper
½ cup minced onion
1 cup Sesame Sauce (previous recipe)

Soak the shiitake mushrooms in warm water for 15 to 20 minutes, or until soft. Squeeze out the excess liquid. Discard the stalks. Finely slice the caps. Soak the cloud ears in warm water for 15 to 20 minutes, or until soft. Rinse in cold water. Drain thoroughly in a colander.

Steep the noodles in 2 quarts of very hot water for 12 to 15 minutes, or until soft. Drain thoroughly. Slice the noodles into 3-inch lengths and set aside.

Heat the oil in a wok or large frying pan. When hot, add the mushrooms, cloud ears, carrot, green pepper, onion, and ½ cup water. Stir-fry for 5 to 6 minutes, or until the carrots are tender. Stir in the Sesame Sauce. Fold in the noodles. Stir-fry for 1 to 2 minutes, or until heated through. Serve immediately.

YIELDS 4 SERVINGS.

Five-grain Rice

OGOK BAP

Traditionally eaten on the first full moon of the lunar year, Taeborum, Five-grain Rice is a nutritious accompaniment to any meal! The dish is composed of red beans (*pat*), black beans, (*kong*), millet (*cha cho*), sweet rice (*chapssal*), and sorghum (*susu*) or rice (*bap*). Steam the rice the conventional way, or simplify the process by using a rice cooker.

> 1 tablespoon red beans
> 1 tablespoon black beans
> 1 tablespoon millet
> 2 cups glutinous rice
> ¼ cup sorghum or short-grain rice
> 1 teaspoon salt, or to taste

Soak the beans in water for a minimum of 3 hours, then drain. In another bowl, soak the millet and rice in water for a minimum of 3 hours, then drain.

In a 2-quart pot of fresh water, bring the beans to a boil. Then simmer for an hour, or until tender. Reserve and measure the liquid. Add enough water to total 3 cups.

Combine the beans, millet, rice, sorghum, and salt in the 3 cups reserved water.

If steaming the grains, bring the ingredients to a boil in a 2-quart pot. Lower the heat, cover, and simmer for 25 minutes, or until the moisture has been absorbed. Remove from the heat and allow to steam for 10 minutes.

If using a rice cooker, place the grains, salt, and water in a 5-cup rice cooker. Follow the cooker's directions.

Remove the grains from the pot or cooker. Fluff with a fork and serve.

YIELDS **4** SERVINGS.

Wood Rabbit

February 14, 1915 to February 2, 1916
February 11, 1975 to January 30, 1976

 Generous with love, you are successful at life.

Auspicious Foods
Spicy soup, noodles, heart of palm, sour flavors.

Bean Sprout and Green Onion Salad

SOOK CHOO NA MOOL

2 tablespoons peanut oil
2 tablespoons rice vinegar
2 tablespoons light soy sauce
½ cup diagonally sliced green onions, plus additional for
 garnish
2 tablespoons chopped pimiento
½ teaspoon ground black pepper, or to taste
1 clove garlic, crushed
2 cups mung bean sprouts
1 tablespoon sesame seeds

Mix the oil, vinegar, soy sauce, green onions, pimiento, pepper, and garlic. Pour mixture over the bean sprouts and toss until the sprouts are lightly coated. Chill for 30 to 45 minutes. Toss salad again. Serve on chilled plates. Garnish with diagonally sliced green onions and sesame seeds.

YIELDS 4 TO 6 SERVINGS.

Pickled Stuffed Cucumber

OI SOBAEGI KIMCHI

9 small pickling cucumbers
2 tablespoons salt
2 cups peeled and julienned daikon (white radish)
2 green onions, chopped (¼ cup)
1 tablespoon minced fresh ginger
1 clove garlic, minced
1 tablespoon chili powder, or to taste
1 tablespoon sugar

Wash and slice cucumbers lengthwise and across, cutting almost to the ends. The cuts will resemble a plus sign (+). Rub 1 tablespoon salt on the cucumbers inside and out and let rest for 30 minutes. Squeeze out excess water.

Combine the daikon with the remaining 1 tablespoon salt, green onions, ginger, garlic, chili powder, and sugar. Divide it equally among the cucumbers, stuffing the mixture into the cavities.

Place the stuffed cucumbers in a clean jar or crock, pressing down firmly. Cover with ½ cup boiling water. Leave overnight at room temperature. Refrigerate in the morning.

The kimchi may be eaten the first morning but will stay crisp for a week in the refrigerator.

YIELDS 9 STUFFED CUCUMBERS.

Fire Rabbit

February 2, 1927 to January 22, 1928
January 29, 1987 to February 16, 1988

 An entrepreneur, you find life an exciting adventure.

Auspicious Foods
Spicy soup, noodles, almonds, bitter flavors.

Cellophane Noodles and Shiitake Mushrooms

CHAP CHAE

Chap chae is Korean for "many vegetables." This is a traditional New Year's Day dish that lends itself to unlimited substitutions. Use whatever vegetables are in season or what you have on hand—and you have the makings of a party!

Meat Seasoning
2 teaspoons soy sauce
2 teaspoons raw or light brown sugar
1 clove garlic, minced
1 teaspoon rice wine vinegar
1 teaspoon sesame oil
⅛ teaspoon ground black pepper, or to taste

Combine all the ingredients and set aside.

Chap chae Seasonings
¼ cup soy sauce
¼ cup sesame oil
¼ cup raw or light brown sugar
1 tablespoon sesame seeds

Combine all the ingredients and set aside.

Chap Chae

8 ounces beef, sliced
¼ pound shiitake mushrooms, sliced (½ cup)
½ cup spinach
1 small onion, sliced (½ cup)
2 green onions, sliced diagonally
2 cloves garlic, crushed
1 medium carrot, peeled and sliced (½ cup)
4 tablespoons sesame oil
*8 ounces dried cellophane noodles (*dang myun*)*
½ teaspoon salt

Combine the beef and mushrooms with the meat seasoning. Set aside.

Blanch the spinach in boiling water for 1 minute or until the leaves wilt slightly. Drain thoroughly.

Stir-fry the onion, green onions, garlic, and carrots in 2 tablespoons of the oil. Remove vegetables and keep warm. Sauté the beef and mushrooms in 2 tablespoons oil. Remove from heat and keep warm.

Add the noodles and salt to 2 quarts boiling water. Cook 4 minutes, or until tender-crisp. Drain thoroughly.

In a large wok, combine the noodles, meat, and vegetable mixtures with the *chap chae* seasoning. Stir-fry for 5 to 6 minutes, or until the flavors have blended and the mixture has heated through. Serve immediately.

YIELDS 6 SERVINGS.

Variations: Substitute broccoli florets, sweet red or green peppers, napa cabbage, leeks, celery, button mushrooms, straw mushrooms, or mustard greens for the vegetables.

Wonton Wrappers

Mandu

3 cups sifted, all-purpose flour
¾ teaspoon salt
2 eggs, beaten

Mix the flour and salt. Form a well in the center for the eggs and ⅔ cup cold water. Combine the ingredients, shaping into a soft ball. Knead the dough for 4 to 5 minutes, or until smooth and elastic. Divide into 4 parts. Roll 1 ball at a time into a 14-inch square about ¹⁄₁₆ inch thick. Use a 3-inch cookie cutter or a glass rim to cut the dough into rounds. Cover the completed wontons with a damp towel while working with the other 3 dough balls. These may be made ahead, wrapped in foil, and frozen.

To cook wontons, wrap each pastry around a teaspoon of filling. Fold the wrapper in half and pinch or crimp the edges, using a drop of water, if necessary, to seal it. Wontons may be boiled in salted water or steamed/stir-fried as pot-stickers.

If boiling the wontons, bring 2 quarts salted water to a boil. Carefully add the dumplings with a slotted spoon. When the dumplings rise to the top, add 1 cup cold water. Do not cover. Allow the water to come to a boil and the dumplings to rise to the top a second time. Carefully remove the dumplings with a slotted spoon.

If steaming/stir-frying the wontons, add 2 tablespoons sesame oil and the dumplings to a wok or skillet. Cover and turn the heat to medium. After 2 to 3 minutes, or when the dumplings are beginning to brown lightly, flip them over to cook the other side. Cover and allow to cook for another 2 to 3 minutes, or until golden brown and firm. If using a meat filling, flip the dumplings over a second time, cover, and allow to steam/fry another 2 to 3 minutes, or until filling is thoroughly cooked.

Yields **36** wrappers.

Earth Rabbit

February 19, 1939 to February 7, 1940
February 16, 1999 to February 4, 2000

 You abound with enthusiasm for life and love.

Auspicious Foods
Spicy soup, noodles, dates, sweet flavors.

Steamed Eggs with Anchovy

This dish is great for a party brunch or company breakfast. Prepare and serve the eggs in individual foil cupcake wrappers. With easy preparation, elegant presentation, and fast cleanup, what could be better?

6 ounces anchovies
3 teaspoons sesame oil
6 eggs, lightly beaten
1 ½ teaspoon rice wine
½ teaspoon salt, or to taste
6 tablespoons julienned sweet red pepper
6 tablespoons finely sliced green onion

Sauté the anchovies in 1 teaspoon sesame oil for 1 to 2 minutes. Combine the eggs, wine, and salt with 1 ½ cups water in a large bowl. Fold in the anchovies.

Spray or rub the insides of 4 foil cupcake wrappers with the remaining 2 teaspoons sesame oil. Spoon in the egg mixture. Garnish the tops with the red pepper and green onion. Place in a steamer or double boiler for 4 to 5 minutes, or until the eggs are set.

Yields 6 servings.

Dragon
BETWEEN SEASONS

Metal Dragon

February 8, 1940 to January 26, 1941
February 5, 2000 to January 23, 2001

 *Ambitious and enthusiastic, you have the golden touch.*

Auspicious Foods
Chicken, soup, bamboo shoots, peaches, spicy flavors.

Barbecuing

An old Korean adage states, "Koreans eat the ox from the hooves to the horns." Although the saying grossly exaggerates the truth, beef has traditionally been so expensive that nothing was wasted. Tripe, chitterlings, and oxtails are still considered delicacies. Sirloin and tenderloin were reserved for special holidays and celebrations.

Traditionally, food was grilled over a charcoal brazier. These braziers consisted of copper-lined wells inside wooden cases, into which charcoal bricks were added. A few of these old braziers can be found in upscale antique shops. Today, people use portable gas grills for picnics or, at home, use unique electric burners designed for that purpose. Many restaurants specializing in grilled food have a gas burner built into each table. However, the purists still use the traditional method since many prefer the flavor of charcoal to that of gas.

To eat *bulgogi* in the traditional way, place a strip or two of barbecued meat in a large lettuce leaf. Add rice, chopped *kimchi*, shredded vegetables, or *doen jang* (soybean paste) for flavor. Eat out of hand as you would a taco.

Barbecued Beef Sirloin

BULGOGI I

1 ½ pounds sirloin
1 medium onion, finely chopped (½ cup)
1 tablespoon sugar
1 tablespoon soy sauce
¼ teaspoon ground black pepper, or to taste
1 teaspoon sesame seeds
3 cloves garlic, minced
3 green onions, minced
1 tablespoon pineapple juice
1 tablespoon sesame oil

Slice the sirloin across the grain into very thin, ½-inch strips. Set aside. Combine all the remaining ingredients in a large bowl. Fold in the beef strips. Cover, refrigerate, and allow to marinate for 2 to 8 hours. Remove the beef from the marinade.

Broil the beef strips or barbeque them on the grill. Barbecue the marinated beef for 2 to 3 minutes on each side in a shallow metal pan over the grill. Brush with the reserved marinade, turning the beef, and cook until done.

YIELDS 1 ½ POUNDS OR 6 SERVINGS.

Barbecued Chicken Breasts

DAK BULGOGI

Try making *dak bulgogi* by substituting chicken breast halves for steak for outdoor grilling or oven broiling.

Barbecued Pork

DOEJI BULGOGI

Try making *doeji bulgogi* by substituting sliced pork for steak when outdoor grilling or oven broiling. Be sure to cook the pork and marinade *thoroughly!*

Barbecued Chitterlings and Tripe

YANG KOBCHANG GUI

Try making *yang kobchang gui* by substituting beef chitterlings and tripe for steak. Be sure to thoroughly clean the chitterlings and tripe. Then slice them into 1 $\frac{1}{2}$-inch pieces. Prepare and grill as you would the *bulgogi*, but increase the garlic to 6 cloves and the green onions to 6 stalks. Barbecue over an electric or charcoal grill.

Barbecued Beef

BULGOGI II

Ko chu jang, a red-pepper paste made from hot peppers, fermented bean powder, and salt is what gives Korean Barbecued Beef its special flavor.

1 ½ pounds flank steak
6 cloves garlic, crushed
8 green onions, thinly sliced
1 tablespoon minced ginger
1 teaspoon ground black pepper, or to taste
½ cup soy sauce
¼ cup sugar
¼ cup rice wine
1 ½ tablespoons ko chu jang *(available in Asian supermarkets)*
  or 1 teaspoon chili pepper, or to taste
2 tablespoons sesame seeds
3 tablespoons sesame oil

Slice the steak across the grain into thin 1-inch strips. Combine the garlic, half the green onions, ginger, black pepper, soy sauce, sugar, wine, and *ko chu jang*. Marinate for at least 2 hours. Remove the meat from the marinade.

Heat the wok and add the sesame seeds, stirring briskly for 30 seconds to 1 minute, or until lightly brown. Be very careful not to scorch the seeds. Remove the seeds and set aside. Add 1 tablespoon oil with ⅓ of the meat mixture. Do not overlap the slices. Stir-fry the steak on high. Set aside and keep warm. Repeat with the remaining steak and oil. Garnish with the freshly toasted sesame seeds and the remaining green onions.

YIELDS 1 ½ POUNDS OR 6 SERVINGS.

Hint: *Bulgogi* can also be broiled in the oven. If preparing the steak for this method, cut the meat into 2 ½- to 3-inch-long, thin strips, reduce the oil to 1 tablespoon, and add it to the marinade. Broil the meat for 2 to 3 minutes on each side.

Hint: Bulgogi can also be barbecued on the grill. If preparing the steak for this method, cut the meat into 2 $\frac{1}{2}$- to 3-inch-long, thin strips, reduce the oil to 1 tablespoon, and add it to the marinade. Cook the marinated beef for 2 to 3 minutes on each side in a shallow metal pan over the grill.

Grilled Short Ribs

6 pounds (about 36), short ribs cut into 6 pieces
1 ¼ cups sugar
1 teaspoon ground black pepper
2 kiwis, peeled and coarsely chopped
1 pear, peeled, cored, and coarsely chopped
½ cup finely chopped onion
4 green onions, finely chopped
½ cup minced garlic (6 to 8 cloves)
2 tablespoons minced fresh ginger
1 cup soy sauce
½ cup rice wine
3 tablespoons sesame seeds
½ cup sesame oil

Rub the ribs with ¼ cup of the sugar and ½ teaspoon of the black pepper. Place in a covered container and refrigerate for 3 hours.

Combine all the remaining ingredients. Pour over the ribs, turning the ribs to coat evenly. Cover and refrigerate for 4 to 5 hours, turning the ribs occasionally to evenly marinate.

Barbecue the ribs on an outdoor grill or broil for 10 to 12 minutes on each side, or until done.

Yields 6 servings.

The Best of Korean Cuisine

Water Dragon

Blessed with both common sense and
a sense of humor, you have it all.

Auspicious Foods
Chicken, soup, bamboo shoots, chestnuts, salty flavors.

Seafood Roll-ups

KIM BAP

Seafood Roll-ups are the Korean answer to Japanese sushi. To make this delectable hors d'oeuvre, you will need to purchase a bamboo sushi mat in an Asian supermarket.

4 eggs, beaten
1 ½ teaspoons salt
2 tablespoons sugar
4 tablespoons sesame oil
1 tablespoon soy sauce
¼ pound ground chuck beef
1 clove garlic, minced
¼ pound fresh spinach (2 cups)
1 cup carrot sticks (¼ by ¼ by 1-inch)
½ cup rice wine vinegar
⅛ teaspoon ground black pepper
4 cups hot, cooked rice
8 sheets dried seaweed (nori; available in
 Asian supermarkets)
1 cup daikon sticks (¼ by ¼ by 1-inch)
Pickled ginger (see recipe, page 121)

Combine the eggs with ¼ teaspoon salt and ½ teaspoon sugar. Sauté in a skillet in 1 tablespoon sesame oil, as if making an omelet.

Fry for 1 to 2 minutes, then flip over and sauté on the other side for 1 to 2 minutes, or until the eggs have set. Remove from pan and slice into $\frac{1}{4}$ by 1-inch strips.

Mix the soy sauce and 1 tablespoon sugar with the ground chuck. Brown the beef mixture and garlic in 2 tablespoons sesame oil.

Blanch the spinach and carrot sticks in 1 quart boiling water for 1 minute. Remove with tongs or a slotted spoon. Rinse in cold water and squeeze out excess water.

In the remaining 1 tablespoon sesame oil and 2 $\frac{1}{2}$ teaspoons sugar, braise the spinach and carrots for 1 to 2 minutes or until tender-crisp.

Add the vinegar and the remaining 1 $\frac{1}{4}$ teaspoons salt and the black pepper to the hot rice. Mix gently but thoroughly. Allow the rice to cool enough to handle comfortably.

Place a sushi mat on a flat surface. Line it with a thin sheet of dried seaweed. On top of the seaweed, layer $\frac{1}{2}$ cup of the rice (evenly spread), a narrow row of meat, egg strips, a bit of spinach, and a strip or two of carrot and daikon. Be sure the layers are thin and even, and leave an extra bit of seaweed overlapping at the edge for securing. Roll up in a jellyroll fashion, pressing as you go. The seaweed, if pressed together, will seal itself. When set, slice it into 4 pinwheel appetizers. Garnish with pickled ginger.

YIELDS 8 ROLLS OR 32 PINWHEEL APPETIZERS.

Hint: Use leftover cooked chicken, pork, fish, crabmeat, or shrimp instead of the beef. Experiment with thin, crisp cucumber or celery strips instead of the daikon.

Wood Dragon

February 16, 1904 to February 3, 1905
February 13, 1964 to February 1, 1965

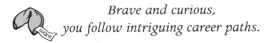 *Brave and curious,*
you follow intriguing career paths.

Auspicious Foods
Chicken, soup, bamboo shoots, heart of palm, sour flavors.

Bamboo Shoots

Bamboo is a member of the grass family. Native to Southeast Asia, bamboo shoots are a good source of potassium and fiber, low in calories, and relatively inexpensive. The shoots of young bamboo plants have many uses: vegetable side dishes, stir-fry ingredients, appetizers, or flavorful additions to soups and salads.

Fresh bamboo shoots have a crisp, firm texture and slightly nutty flavor. The shoots are pale golden-brown in color and about 10 inches long. Fresh shoots keep well in the refrigerator for up to a week if tightly wrapped in plastic.

Canned bamboo shoots are available in Asian supermarkets. Though not as flavorful or crisp as fresh shoots, they are an acceptable substitute. Canned bamboo shoots are tan in color, sliced, and precooked. To remove the metallic tin taste, rinse the shoots in cold water and drain thoroughly.

Bamboo Shoots with Carrot Sesame Dressing

½ pound fresh bamboo shoots
⅛ teaspoon salt, or to taste

Use a paring knife to peel the outer skin. Cook the pale inner cores in salted, boiling water for 10 to 12 minutes, or until tender, and drain. Chill. Slice into thin medallions, julienne, or dice the shoots. Serve with Carrot Sesame Dressing (recipe follows).

YIELDS 2 SERVINGS.

Hint: Double the recipe. Add leftover bamboo shoots to stir-fried dishes, soups, or salads for a crunchy texture and a slightly nutty flavor.

Carrot Sesame Dressing

¼ cup soy sauce
2 tablespoons rice wine
1 tablespoon lime juice
1 tablespoon finely minced carrot
2 tablespoons sesame oil
½ tablespoon sugar
1 green onion, minced

Combine all the ingredients thoroughly.

YIELDS 1 CUP.

Fire Dragon

February 3, 1916 to January 22, 1917
January 31, 1976 to February 17, 1977

 A natural-born leader, you are powerful and persuasive.

Auspicious Foods
Chicken, soup, bamboo shoots, almonds, bitter flavors.

Sautéed Oriental Eggplant

GAJI NAMUL

> *2 ounce dried shrimp*
> *4 teaspoons raw or brown sugar*
> *2 pounds (4 medium) Oriental eggplants*
> *4 tablespoons sesame oil*
> *2 cloves garlic, minced*
> *2 medium tomatoes*
> *2 teaspoons salt, or to taste*
> *½ teaspoon ground black pepper, or to taste*
> *½ teaspoon red pepper powder, or to taste*
> *2 tablespoons rice wine*

Rehydrate the dried shrimp in ½ cup warm water with 1 teaspoon sugar for 30 minutes. Drain.

Cut eggplant diagonally into ½-inch slices. Using a wok or large frying pan, heat the oil. Add the shrimp, eggplant, and garlic. Sauté for 2 to 3 minutes.

Peel and slice each tomato into 6 wedges. Add the tomato, salt, black and red peppers, wine, and remaining 3 teaspoons sugar to the eggplant mixture. Stir-fry for 5 to 6 minutes, or until the eggplant is tender and the liquid has been absorbed.

YIELDS **8** SERVINGS.

Earth Dragon

January 23, 1928 to February 9, 1929
February 17, 1988 to February 5, 1989

 Kind and caring, you are surrounded by friends.

Auspicious Foods
Chicken, soup, bamboo shoots, dates, sweet flavors.

Steamed Rice

BAP

In Korea, rice is eaten with every meal. It can be made into porridge for breakfast. Mixed with vegetables, rice is a lunch mainstay, and it can be combined with beans or barley for a hearty dinner.

Rice, soup, and *kimchi* make up the tri-cornered foundation of a Korean meal. *Banchan*, side dishes, may be added as generously as desired.

Following is a recipe for the traditional method of steaming rice. For consistently perfect rice, a rice cooker is suggested.

1 ½ cups raw, short-grain rice

Add the rice to 2 ¼ cups water in a 2-quart pot. Bring to a boil, then reduce the heat, cover, and simmer for 20 to 22 minutes, or until the liquid is absorbed.

Remove the pot from the heat. Still covered, let the rice steam for 10 minutes. (Don't peek!) Fluff with a fork or chopsticks and serve immediately.

YIELDS 3 ½ CUPS.

Snake
SUMMER

Metal Snake

January 27, 1941 to February 14, 1942
January 24, 2001 to February 11, 2002

Your eye on the future,
you work hard today to enjoy tomorrow.

Auspicious Foods
Shark, Chinese cabbage, peaches, spicy flavors.

Frosty Cucumber Soup

OI NAENG KUK

Frosty cucumber soup refreshes the palate during the steamiest summer days. Chill the soup bowls in the freezer for 2 hours before ladling in the light soup.

4 small cucumbers, thinly sliced
1 tablespoon blanched seaweed, optional
1 tablespoon rice wine vinegar
½ tablespoon sugar
½ tablespoon soy sauce
½ teaspoon minced garlic
½ teaspoon salt, or to taste
⅛ teaspoon ground black pepper
¼ cup crushed ice
1 tablespoon sesame seeds
1 green onion, thinly sliced

Combine 2 cups boiled, chilled water with the cucumbers, seaweed, vinegar, sugar, soy sauce, garlic, salt, and pepper. Allow to stand for 20 to 30 minutes, stirring occasionally, for the flavors to marry. Ladle into 2 icy bowls. Garnish with a mound of crushed ice in the center. Lightly sprinkle with sesame seeds and green onion slices.

YIELDS 2 SERVINGS.

Water Snake

February 14, 1953 to February 2, 1954

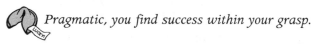 *Pragmatic, you find success within your grasp.*

Auspicious Foods
Shark, Chinese cabbage, chestnuts, salty flavors.

Chili Kimchi

KIMCHI

1 large head (2 pounds) napa cabbage
3 tablespoons salt
6 red chili peppers
6 green onions
6 cloves garlic
1 tablespoon grated fresh ginger
¼ teaspoon cayenne pepper, or to taste

Cut cabbage into 1-inch slices. Dissolve 2 tablespoons salt in enough water to cover the cabbage slices in any nonreactive container: a large crockery or glass jar. Allow the cabbage to steep in the salted water for 18 to 24 hours at room temperature. Rinse the cabbage well, drain, and set aside.

Chop the peppers (including the seeds), green onions, garlic, and ginger, and mix with the remaining 1 tablespoon salt and the cayenne pepper. Add the chopped pepper mixture to 1 cup water in a nonreactive container. Pack the cabbage, adding enough water to cover, and gently stir the mixture. Refrigerate for several days before serving. Keeps up to a week if refrigerated. Remove the kimchi from its liquid before serving.

YIELDS 2 POUNDS.

Wood Snake

February 4, 1905 to January 24, 1906
February 2, 1965 to January 20, 1966

 Chase your dreams until you reach success.

Auspicious Foods
Shark, Chinese cabbage, heart of palm, sour flavors.

Pickled Eggplant

KAJI KIMCHI

½ pound (1 medium) oriental eggplant (available in
    Asian supermarkets)
½ teaspoon salt
¼ teaspoon seeded and julienned green chili
1 clove garlic, crushed
1 tablespoon minced fresh ginger
2 green onions, the green part cut into 3-inch-long strips,
    the white part sliced
1 teaspoon hot red chili flakes
1 tablespoon julienned onion

Add the eggplant and salt to 2 cups boiling water in a 2-quart saucepan. Lower the heat and simmer for 2 to 3 minutes, turning the eggplant occasionally, or until the eggplant is tender-crisp. Remove, drain, allow to cool, and cut into equal lengths of 3 to 4 inches. Cut a deep cross in one end of each piece, so that the filling may be inserted. Set aside.

Combine the green chili, garlic, ginger, green onions, chili flakes, and onion. Open the cut in each eggplant and press in about ¼ cup of the filling, taking care to distribute it equally among the eggplant pieces. Place the stuffed eggplant in a glass or plastic container that has a tight cover. Cover the container and put it in a cool but not refrigerated spot for 1 day to marinate. Serve or refrigerate. The kimchi is best eaten during the first 3 days if you prefer a lighter flavor since the heat intensifies daily as the mixture ferments. It may be refrigerated for up to 1 week.

YIELDS 2 CUPS.

Pickled Cabbage with Ginger

SAENG KANG KIMCHI

9 pounds (about 3 medium) napa cabbages
½ cup salt
3 pounds (about 2 medium) daikon (white radishes),
peeled and shredded
2 tablespoons minced fresh ginger
3 cloves garlic, minced
6 green onions, coarsely chopped
2 tablespoons red pepper powder
2 tablespoons raw or light brown sugar

Cut the cabbage into 1 ½-inch squares. Place it in a large container, layering it with a sprinkling of salt. Set aside for 3 hours, or until the cabbage becomes limp. Rinse the leaves with water. Drain thoroughly. Add the remaining ingredients and mix well. Store in a gallon-sized glass jar or ceramic crock. (Plastic containers will stain and hold the pungent aroma.) Set aside in a cool (but not refrigerated) place for up to 3 days, or until it ferments. It is ready when it tastes a little sour. Refrigerate to stop the fermentation. Eat immediately or store up to a week in the refrigerator.

YIELDS 1 GALLON.

Korean Cucumber Salad

6 small cucumbers
4 green onions, thinly sliced
1 tablespoon sesame oil
1 tablespoon rice wine vinegar
1/2 teaspoon red chili powder, or to taste
1/4 teaspoon salt
1/2 teaspoon sugar

Trim both ends of the cucumbers and score, creating 2 long, narrow gouges in each cucumber to produce a design. Thinly slice the cucumbers diagonally. Combine all the ingredients and toss to coat evenly. Serve cold or at room temperature.

Yields 2 servings.

Piquant Shark and Shellfish with Vegetables

SENGSUN MEUNTANG

1 pound shark or cod fillets
4 bay scallops
12 cooked mussels
8 cooked prawns
1 medium onion, sliced into eighths
20 button mushrooms, rinsed
1 sweet red pepper, julienned
1 clove garlic, minced
1 teaspoon chili pepper, or to taste
1 tablespoon chili sauce, or to taste
1 teaspoon salt, or to taste
4 green onions, sliced diagonally
1 medium zucchini, sliced into eighths
½ cup cilantro leaves, stems removed

Cut the fish into bite-sized pieces. Remove the scallops, mussels, and prawns from their shells.

Add the fish to 2 cups boiling water. Add all the ingredients except the cilantro, bring to a boil, lower the heat, and simmer for 6 to 9 minutes, or until the fish, shellfish, and vegetables are tender but not overcooked.

Divide the ingredients and broth equally among 4 warmed bowls. Garnish with aromatic cilantro leaves and serve steaming hot.

YIELDS 4 SERVINGS.

Fire Snake

January 23, 1917 to February 10, 1918
February 18, 1977 to February 6, 1978

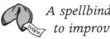 *A spellbinding raconteur, you need
to improve your listening skills.*

Auspicious Foods
Shark, Chinese cabbage, almonds, bitter flavors.

Stuffed Red Peppers

KOCHU CHON

2 (2-inch-long) sweet red peppers
4 ounces ground round
¼ teaspoon salt
1 tablespoon soy sauce
1 green onion, minced
1 clove garlic, minced
¼ teaspoon ground black pepper, or to taste
¼ cup firm tofu, drained
1 tablespoon flour
1 egg
1 tablespoon sesame oil

Slice the peppers lengthwise. Remove the stems and seeds.

Thoroughly combine the beef with ⅛ teaspoon salt, the soy sauce, green onion, garlic, and black pepper. Crumble the tofu into the mixture and mix well.

Stuff the peppers with the meat mixture. Dredge with the flour. Beat the egg with the remaining ⅛ teaspoon salt. Dip the peppers into the egg.

Sauté the stuffed peppers in the oil, turning to cook evenly. Pan-fry for 8 to 10 minutes, or until the meat is done. Serve with Soy Sauce Dip (recipe follows).

YIELDS 2 SERVINGS.

Soy Sauce Dip

YANG NYOM JANG

¼ cup soy sauce
2 green onions, thinly sliced
½ tablespoon sesame oil
½ teaspoon sesame seeds
⅛ teaspoon ground black pepper
Dash of chili powder, optional

Combine all the ingredients. Use as a sauce for fried foods.

YIELDS ½ CUP.

Earth Snake

February 10, 1929 to January 29, 1930
February 6, 1989 to January 26, 1990

*Intriguing and playful,
you attract friends and admirers easily.*

Auspicious Foods
Shark, Chinese cabbage, dates, sweet flavors.

Pumpkin Fritters with Pine Nut Sauce

*½ pound pumpkin
1 egg, beaten
½ teaspoon salt
¼ teaspoon pepper
¼ cup sifted all-purpose flour
1 tablespoon sesame oil*

Peel the pumpkin and remove seeds. Slice it into ¼-inch wedges. Dip the slices in the beaten egg. Combine the salt, pepper, and flour. Dredge the pumpkin in the seasoned flour. Add the oil to a hot skillet and sauté the pumpkin wedges until both sides are golden brown. Serve with Pine Nut Sauce. (See recipe below.)

Yields 2 servings.

Pine Nut Sauce

1 tablespoon soy sauce
1 tablespoon water
1 tablespoon rice vinegar
1 tablespoon ground pine nuts

Combine all the ingredients, stirring to completely blend.

YIELDS ½ CUP.

Horse
SUMMER

Metal Horse

January 30, 1930 to February 16, 1931
January 27, 1990 to February 14, 1991

 Intuitive and resourceful, you adjust to change with lightning speed.

Auspicious Foods
Parsley, ginger root, peaches, spicy flavors.

Ginger

SAENG KANG

Ginger, the spice of life, enhances any recipe. The root of this sweet-sharp herb is so versatile, it can be used fresh, crystallized, pickled, or ground.

Fresh: Store fresh ginger in the refrigerator. To use, peel the thin skin with a paring knife. Mince or grate the ginger for even flavor distribution or slice into extremely thin "coins" for more robust flavor. Try fresh ginger to infuse a curious, sweet-sharp flavor. Pair freshly minced ginger with garlic for fragrant stir-fried dishes.

Powdered: Dried ginger is convenient to use and store, but its long shelf life diminishes its fire. A teaspoon or two added to soups, squash, or root vegetables lends a distinctive tang. Use also in spice rubs for fish, pork, and chicken. Generally 1 teaspoon of dried ginger equals 3 teaspoons of freshly grated ginger.

Candied or crystallized: Purchase crystallized ginger in an Asian supermarket or gourmet food department, although it is easy to make your own (see recipe below). Sweet, spicy, and pungent, it is delicious alone, but try it in desserts, sweet sauces, or candied fruit dishes for tangy bursts of flavor.

Crystallized Ginger

1 ¼ cups sugar
1 cup fresh ginger

Combine 1 cup sugar and ½ cup water in a saucepan. Bring to a boil then lower the flame. Peel and coarsely chop the fresh ginger. Immerse the ginger in the syrup. Simmer for 15 minutes or until translucent. Remove from the syrup with a slotted spoon. Reserve syrup for other use. Arrange ginger pieces on cake rack over paper until almost dry. Roll in ¼ cup sugar and place on parchment paper to dry thoroughly.

YIELDS 1 CUP.

Hint: Brush purchased, warm pound cake with reserved sugar syrup. Garnish generously with bits of crystallized or candied ginger.

Pickled: Purchase pickled ginger in an Asian supermarket or gourmet food department, although it is easy to make your own (see recipe below). It is used most often as an accompaniment to sushi and sashimi. Try it with julienned green onions as a garnish for baked fish.

Pickled Ginger

¼ pound fresh ginger
1 cup unseasoned rice vinegar
¼ cup cider vinegar
½ cup sugar
2 teaspoons kosher salt

Bring 2 quarts water to a boil. Peel the ginger and slice into paper-thin coins, cutting crosswise, against the grain. Immerse the ginger in the boiling water. Blanch for 2 minutes. Remove with a slotted spoon and drain in a colander. Place ginger in a large, clean glass jar or plastic container.

Combine the vinegars, sugar, and salt in a nonaluminum pot. Stir over moderate heat just until the sugar and salt dissolve. Pour over the ginger and allow to cool completely. Cover and refrigerate for 24 hours. Keeps up to 2 weeks in refrigerator.

YIELDS 2 CUPS.

Hints: Serve pickled ginger with fish, cold cuts, and vegetables. Use the sweet/sour juice in soups and sauces.

Parsley

Use the flat leaf variety of parsley for the most pungent flavor in cooking, although curly parsley works well with cold dishes. Use fresh parsley when possible, but dried parsley will do in a pinch. Substitute 1 tablespoon fresh parsley for 1 teaspoon of the dried leaves.

Hints: Bundle 6 or 7 fresh parsley sprigs together. Simmer in stews or soups. Use the parsley bundles as herbal brushes for spreading sauces onto meats. Sprinkle freshly chopped parsley leaves over noodles.

Water Horse

February 15, 1942 to February 4, 1943

 Your cheerfulness and patience reward you with big dividends.

Auspicious Foods
Parsley, ginger root, chestnuts, salty flavors.

Steamed Rice with Chestnuts

BAP

The following recipe is the traditional method of steaming rice. For consistently perfect rice, a rice cooker is suggested.

12 chestnuts
1 ½ cups raw, short-grain rice

Peel the chestnuts and cut them into halves. Add the chestnuts and rice to 2 ½ cups water in a 2-quart pot. Bring to a boil, then reduce the heat, cover, and simmer for 22 to 24 minutes, or until the liquid is absorbed.

Remove the pot from the heat. Still covered, let the rice steam for 10 minutes. (Don't peek!) Fluff with a fork or chopsticks and serve immediately.

YIELDS 3 ½ CUPS.

Wood Horse

February 3, 1954 to January 23, 1955

Possessing animal magnetism,
you attract many admirers.

Auspicious Foods
Parsley, ginger root, heart of palm, sour flavors.

Melon Pear Nectar

3 bell peppers, seeded and sliced
4 ounces (about ½ melon) cantaloupe, cubed
2 ounces (1 small) Asian pear, sliced
4 tablespoons fresh parsley
1 teaspoon fresh lemon juice
Parsley sprigs for garnish
Thin lemon slices for garnish

Add the ingredients to a juicer for a refreshing drink. If desired, serve over crushed ice. Garnish with a parsley sprig and thin lemon slice.

YIELDS **8** OUNCES.

Fire Horse

January 25, 1906 to February 12, 1907
January 21, 1966 to February 8, 1967

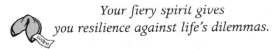

*Your fiery spirit gives
you resilience against life's dilemmas.*

Auspicious Foods
Parsley, ginger root, almonds, bitter flavors.

Hale n' Hearty Kale Juice

*4 ounces kale
1 stalk celery, sliced
1 medium apple, sliced
1 orange, peeled
Orange twist, optional garnish*

Add the ingredients to a juicer for a refreshing tonic. If desired,
serve over crushed ice with a twist of orange.

YIELDS **8** OUNCES.

Lemon Lettuce Cooler

*6 ounces (about ¹/₂ head) iceberg lettuce leaves
¹/₂ medium apple, sliced
¹/₂ carrot, peeled and sliced
1 teaspoons fresh lemon juice
Lemon twist, optional garnish*

Add the ingredients to a juicer. If desired, serve over crushed ice
with a twist of lemon.

YIELDS **8** OUNCES.

Earth Horse

February 11, 1918 to January 31, 1919
February 7, 1978 to January 27, 1979

 You stride through life as graceful and regal as a stallion.

Auspicious Foods
Parsley, ginger root, dates, sweet flavors.

Mandarin Orange Celery Juice

3 stalks celery
1 carrot, peeled and sliced
½ medium apple, sliced
1 small mandarin orange, peeled
Celery leaf, optional garnish

Add all the ingredients to a juicer except for one orange segment and a leafy sprig of celery. If desired, serve over crushed ice. Garnish with the orange segment and celery sprig.

YIELDS **8** OUNCES.

Orange Beer

½ cup orange segments, skins removed
½ cup beer
Orange twist, optional garnish

Add orange segments to a blender. Using the pulse setting, blend just until the segments become juice. Mix with beer. If desired, garnish with a twist of orange.

YIELDS **8** OUNCES.

Sheep

BETWEEN SEASONS

Metal Sheep

February 17, 1931 to February 5, 1932
February 15, 1991 to February 3, 1992

 Free-spirited, beware of gambling and casual trysts.

Auspicious Foods
Sweet potatoes, cellophane noodles, peaches, spicy flavors.

Spicy Fish Chowder

MAEWUN TANG

Maewun tang is the Korean equivalent of bouillabaisse. Many specialty seafood restaurants that offer this soup encourage guests to select fish from several aquariums. Popular fish for *maewun tang* include perch, sea bass, red snapper, cod, yellow corvina, globefish, croakers, pollacks, and even freshwater fish like carp or catfish. It can also be made with crabs, shrimp, or clams. When cooking it at home, use leftover bits of fish and shellfish, creating a new dish each time you make the soup.

Because of the soup's spiciness, it is best to eat *maewun tang* by placing a spoonful of rice in your mouth, followed by a small spoonful of soup. Incidentally, this is a popular side dish when drinking. For this purpose, create the soup from raw fish and use more *ko chu jang* or red bean paste. It is believed that the fiery spice clears the head between drinks.

1 pound fish (perch, sea bass, red snapper, cod, or catfish)
4 jumbo shrimp
2 squid, optional
2 tablespoons minced fresh ginger
4 cloves garlic, minced
½ cup coarsely chopped onion (1 medium)
2 cups cubed daikon (white radish; available in Asian
   supermarkets)
4 sweet red peppers, sliced
1 tablespoon chili powder, or to taste
1 teaspoon ko chu jang* *(available in Asian supermar-*
   kets), or to taste
2 tablespoons sesame oil
4 cups beef stock
1 teaspoon salt, or to taste
2 tablespoons rice wine
2 tablespoons coarsely chopped fresh mugwort♦, optional
4 green onions, slivered

Scale and clean fish. Filet and remove any remaining bones. Cut
into 1-inch cubes. Shell and devein the shrimp. Clean and slice the
squid into ¼-inch rings. Add the fish and ginger to 1 quart boiling water. Blanch for 1 to 2 minutes. Remove the fish, drain, and
set aside.

Stir-fry the shrimp, squid, garlic, onion, daikon, sweet peppers,
chili powder, and *ko chu jang* in the sesame oil for 4 to 5 minutes,
or until the shrimp are pink and the sliced squid has become tender rings.

Add the beef stock, salt, and rice wine. Bring to a boil. Add the fish,
lower the heat, and simmer for 12 to 15 minutes, or until the fish is
tender. Add the mugwort during the last minute, cooking only long
enough to blanch its tender leaves. Serve the chowder steaming hot
in earthenware bowls. Garnish with slivered green onions.

YIELDS 4 SERVINGS.

Ko chu jang, or red bean paste, is used for seasoning soups, stews, and dipping sauces. Fiery hot, it is made from fermented red bean paste powder, glutinous rice, red pepper powder, and salt.

•Mugwort, a common herb in Korean cookery, has a refreshing flavor and texture, similar to that of parsley. The herb is especially popular in seafood chowders because it dispels any fishy aroma.

Water Sheep

February 5, 1943 to January 24, 1944

Charming and irresistible, you must resist the urge to take advantage of people.

Auspicious Foods
Sweet potatoes, cellophane noodles, chestnuts, salty flavors.

Stir-Fried Snow Peas and Green Beans

1 clove garlic, minced
1 teaspoon minced fresh ginger
$\frac{1}{4}$ cup sesame oil
$\frac{1}{2}$ cup vegetable or beef broth
1 tablespoon soy sauce, or to taste
$\frac{1}{2}$ pound fresh snow peas, trimmed and strings removed
$\frac{1}{2}$ pound green beans, trimmed and sliced diagonally into
    $\frac{1}{2}$ -inch pieces
2 carrots, pared and sliced diagonally into $\frac{1}{2}$-inch pieces
4 stalks celery, sliced diagonally into $\frac{1}{2}$-inch pieces

Combine the garlic, ginger, and oil in a hot wok. Stir-fry for 1 minute. Add the broth, soy sauce, and vegetables. Stir to coat, cover, and simmer vegetables for 2 to 3 minutes, or until the carrots are crisp-tender.

YIELDS 4 SERVINGS.

Shiitake Mushrooms and Sprouts with Cilantro

Cilantro, also known as Chinese parsley, adds a robust flavor similar to that of sage and citrus. Prepare it by rinsing well and gently removing the tender leaves from the stems. Sprigs or whole or chopped leaves may be used, depending on the recipe.

> 2 cups sliced shiitake mushrooms
> 4 cups mung bean sprouts
> 1/4 cup plus 3 tablespoons chopped cilantro
> 1/4 cup sesame oil
> 2 tablespoons soy sauce, or to taste
> 1/2 teaspoon cornstarch

Rinse the mushrooms and pat dry. Stir-fry the vegetables and 1/4 cup cilantro in the sesame oil quickly at a high temperature, stirring the vegetables constantly to prevent burning. Combine the soy sauce and cornstarch, adding a little water if necessary, to form a thin paste. Whisk the mixture into the vegetables, stirring to coat them evenly. Serve immediately, garnishing with 3 tablespoons cilantro.

YIELDS 4 SERVINGS.

Tomato Juice Korean-Style

> 1 medium tomato, peeled
> 1/2 carrot, peeled and sliced
> 1 teaspoon sesame seed
> Dash soy sauce
> Cherry tomato, optional

Add 1/2 cup water and all the ingredients to a juicer except one thin carrot slice and the cherry tomato. If desired, serve the tomato juice over crushed ice. Garnish with the carrot slice and cherry tomato.

YIELDS 8 OUNCES.

Wood Sheep

January 24, 1955 to February 11, 1956

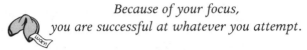

Because of your focus,
you are successful at whatever you attempt.

Auspicious Foods
Sweet potatoes, cellophane noodles, heart of palm, sour flavors.

Cellophane Noodles

DANG MYUN

Cellophane noodles, also known as transparent noodles or Chinese vermicelli, are unusually fine noodles made from mung beans. They are colorless and almost tasteless, but they quickly absorb the flavors of the food with which they are prepared. What makes them unique is their pliable and elastic texture, the perfect complement to the firm textures of hot pot meats. Chinese vermicelli can be simmered, steamed, deep-fried, or used in stir-fry dishes.

16 ounces cellophane noodles

Follow the package's instructions for preparation, or add noodles to 2 quarts salted, boiling water. Cook for 1 to 2 minutes, or until tender-crisp. Drain thoroughly.

YIELDS 4 CUPS.

Seafood "Sausage"

SUNDAE

> 4 medium squids
> 2 tablespoons all-purpose flour
> 1 pound extra-firm tofu
> 1/2 pound ground beef
> 8 ounces bean sprouts
> 4 eggs
> 4 bell green peppers, coarsely chopped
> 4 sweet red peppers, coarsely chopped
> 1/2 cup coarsely chopped green onion
> 1/4 cup coarsely chopped garlic
> 1/2 teaspoon salt, or to taste
> 1/4 teaspoon ground black pepper, or to taste
> 1 lemon, thinly sliced
> Parsley sprigs

Clean the squids thoroughly. Rinse under running water and pat dry with a paper towel. Dust the insides of the squids with flour. Drain the tofu. If necessary, place it between cheesecloth or paper towels and squeeze out any excess water. Combine the tofu with the beef, sprouts, eggs, peppers, onion, garlic, salt, and pepper. Stuff the squids with the tofu mixture. Weave a skewer through the open end of each squid to "sew" it shut.

Place the stuffed seafood in a steamer or double boiler. Cover and steam for 12 to 15 minutes, or until the seafood is tender and white, and the beef is no longer pink.

Carefully remove the seafood with tongs. When cool enough to handle, slice the "sausage" into 1/2-inch rounds. Garnish with lemon slices and parsley sprigs.

YIELDS 8 SERVINGS.

Fire Sheep

February 13, 1907 to February 1, 1908
February 9, 1967 to January 29, 1968

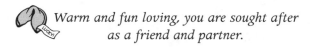 *Warm and fun loving, you are sought after*
as a friend and partner.

Auspicious Foods
Sweet potatoes, cellophane noodles, almonds, bitter flavors.

Grapefruit Cabbage Cooler

2 green outer cabbage leaves
4 ounces grapefruit segments (1 cup)
1 teaspoon honey, or to taste
Lemon twist, optional garnish

Add the ingredients to a blender with ½ cup water. If desired, serve over crushed ice. Garnish with a twist of lemon.

YIELDS **8** OUNCES.

Watermelon and Pineapple Juice

4 ounces watermelon cubes (½ cup)
4 ounces pineapple chunks (½ cup)
1 teaspoon lemon juice

Reserving 1 watermelon cube and 1 pineapple chunk, add the remaining ingredients to a blender. If desired, serve over crushed ice. Garnish with a skewer threaded with the watermelon cube and pineapple chunk.

YIELDS **8** OUNCES.

Earth Sheep

February 1, 1919 to February 19, 1920
January 28, 1979 to February 15, 1980

*No regrets of yesterday; no fears of tomorrow,
you live life to its fullest.*

Auspicious Foods
Sweet potatoes, cellophane noodles, dates, sweet flavors.

Frothy Banana Egg Sunrise

1 banana
1 raw egg
6 ounces soy milk or skim milk
1 teaspoon sugar

Add the ingredients to a blender. Whirl to the consistency of a frothy milkshake.

YIELDS 8 OUNCES.

Monkey

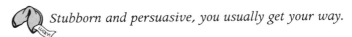

AUTUMN

Metal Monkey

February 20, 1920 to February 7, 1921
February 16, 1980 to February 4, 1981

Stubborn and persuasive, you usually get your way.

Auspicious Foods
Duck, rice, peaches, spicy flavors.

Red Peppers and Potatoes

GAM ZA CHORIM

3 cups potatoes
½ teaspoon salt
4 sweet red peppers, coarsely chopped
½ cup soy sauce
½ cup raw sugar or brown sugar
3 cloves garlic, minced
1 tablespoon rice vinegar
1 tablespoon sesame oil
1 tablespoon sesame seeds

Peel the potatoes and cut into ½-inch cubes. Set aside.

Combine the salt, peppers, soy sauce, sugar, garlic, and vinegar with ¾ cup water in a 2-quart pot. Bring to a boil, then cover and lower the heat. Stirring occasionally, simmer for 6 to 8 minutes, or until the peppers are tender. Add the potatoes, cover, and simmer for 30 minutes, or until the potatoes are tender and the liquid has been absorbed. Check often. If necessary, add another tablespoon or two of water to prevent the vegetables from scorching.

Remove the vegetables from the heat. Gently fold in the sesame oil, creating a red swirl of peppers through the tender potatoes. Spoon mixture into a serving bowl, sprinkle with sesame seeds, and serve immediately.

YIELDS 8 SERVINGS.

Water Monkey

February 6, 1932 to January 25, 1933
February 4, 1992 to January 22, 1993

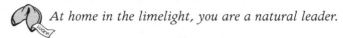 *At home in the limelight, you are a natural leader.*

Auspicious Foods
Duck, rice, chestnuts, salty flavors.

Oxtail Soup

Sokkori Gom Tang

> *1 pound oxtails*
> *1 tablespoon sliced ginger*
> *4 green onions, thinly sliced*
> *1 teaspoon salt, or to taste*
> *4 cloves garlic, minced*
> *¾ pound daikon (white radish)*
>   *or ¾ pound potatoes*
> *1 teaspoon sesame seeds*
> *¼ teaspoon ground black pepper, or to taste*
> *1 teaspoon sesame oil*

Slice oxtails into uniform-length pieces. Rinse well. Combine with the ginger, half the sliced green onions, and 2 quarts salted water. Bring to a boil. Lower the heat, spoon off the foam, and add the garlic. Simmer for 1 ½ hours.

Slice the daikon or potatoes into 2-inch squares (about 3 cups). Add to the oxtails and simmer for another 30 minutes, or until the vegetables are tender and the meat separates easily from the bone. Remove the soup from the heat. Stir in the sesame seeds, pepper, and sesame oil. Ladle into warm soup bowls and garnish with the remaining green onion slices. Serve piping hot.

YIELDS 8 CUPS.

Wood Monkey

January 25, 1944 to February 12, 1945

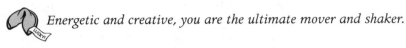 *Energetic and creative, you are the ultimate mover and shaker.*

Auspicious Foods
Duck, rice, heart of palm, sour flavors.

Pork and Cabbage Pinwheels

In this colorful and flavorful dish, pork and cabbage are rolled into tangy white and green rounds that resemble pinwheels.

Crown daisy is a member of the chrysanthemum family. An aromatic herb, it tastes similar to spinach.

1 pound (1 small head) cabbage leaves
½ cup crown daisy leaves or fresh spinach leaves
1 pound boneless fresh pork, sliced paper thin
6 cloves garlic, crushed
3 tablespoon minced fresh ginger
¼ teaspoon salt, or to taste
⅛ teaspoon white ground pepper, or to taste
¼ cup soy paste (available in Asian supermarkets)
⅛ teaspoon chili pepper, or to taste
¼ cup mayonnaise
1 tablespoon sesame seeds
1 tablespoon sesame oil

Rinse the cabbage and crown daisy leaves and pat dry. Place a 12-inch length of aluminum foil on a flat surface. Arrange the cabbage leaves on the foil and the crown daisy leaves on top of the cabbage. Overlap the pork slices on the bed of crown daisy. Sprinkle half the garlic, all the ginger, salt, and white pepper on the pork. Roll up the pork and cabbage. Roll the foil around the mixture, closing the top and both ends securely. Pierce the foil pouch 2 or 3 times with a fork to allow the steam to escape. Lower carefully into a steamer or double boiler. Cover and steam for 40 minutes, or until the pork is completely cooked, showing no hint of pink color. While the pork and cabbage roll is steaming, mix the sauce. Combine the remaining garlic with the soy paste, chili pepper, mayonnaise, sesame seeds, and sesame oil. Mix thoroughly.

Remove the roll with tongs and set aside until cool enough to handle. Remove the foil. Slice the roll into 8 rounds. Arrange on a platter, drizzle with the sauce, and serve immediately.

YIELDS 8 APPETIZER OR 4 ENTRÉE SERVINGS.

Hint: Purchase wafer-thin slices of pork at Asian supermarkets, or place fresh pork in the freezer until semi-frozen. Very firm pork is easily sliced thin, especially if using an electric slicer. Remember to clean all surfaces that come into contact with raw pork with hot, soapy water.

Alternative: Instead of steaming the foil-wrapped pork mixture, grill it.

Sautéed Zucchini and Loofah

Loofah, a source for bath sponges, is actually a delectable vegetable while it is still fresh and tender, resembling squash in both texture and taste. When purchasing loofah, choose firm, unblemished vegetables with dark, outer skins.

> *1 pound zucchini*
> *1 pound loofah (available at Oriental markets),*
>   *or summer squash*
> *½ cup sesame oil*
> *4 cloves garlic, minced*
> *2 tablespoon soy sauce, or to taste*

Wash the vegetables. Score the zucchini with a fork and slice diagonally into ½-inch slices. Peel the loofah and cut diagonally into ½-inch slices. Combine with the oil and garlic and stir-fry over high heat for 1 to 2 minutes. Add the soy sauce and ¼ cup water. Cover and steam for 2 to 3 minutes, or until the vegetable slices are tender yet crisp.

YIELDS 8 SERVINGS.

Fire Monkey

February 12, 1956 to January 30, 1957

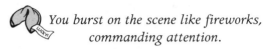 *You burst on the scene like fireworks,*
commanding attention.

Auspicious Foods
Duck, rice, almonds, bitter flavors.

Water Kimchi

Na Bak Kimchi

This thin kimchi ferments in a day and is eaten with a spoon.

> *16 ounces napa cabbage (available in Asian*
>   *supermarkets)*
> *16 ounces daikon (white radish)*
> *2 tablespoons salt*
> *2 green onions*
> *6 banana peppers*
> *4 cloves garlic, sliced*
> *1 tablespoon thinly sliced fresh ginger*
> *1 1/2 tablespoons sugar*
> *1 teaspoon cayenne pepper*

Using the white portion of the napa cabbage, slice into 1-inch pieces. Reserve the green portion for another use. Peel the daikon and cut into 1/2 by 1-inch cubes. Sprinkle the cabbage and radish with the salt. Allow the vegetables to set for 15 minutes and then lightly rinse under running water. Slice the green onions diagonally into 1-inch pieces. Remove the stems and seeds from the peppers and slice lengthwise into 4 strips.

Combine the vegetables with the garlic, ginger, sugar, and 5 cups warm water in a large glass container or crock. Place the cayenne pepper in a cheesecloth or paper towel pouch. Swish the packet in the water once or twice until it imparts a light pink color to the water. Remove the packet.

Cover the container and leave at room temperature for 24 hours to allow fermentation. Refrigerate and serve in chilled cups with soup spoons.

YIELDS 2 QUARTS.

Earth Monkey

February 3, 1908 to January 21, 1909
January 30, 1968 to February 16, 1969

Optimistic and opportunistic,
you find success where others see only failure.

Auspicious Foods
Duck, rice, dates, sweet flavors.

Stir-Fried Rice Cake

TTOK BOKKEE

This dish is very popular at street vendors' carts. School children love it as an after-school snack as much as adults enjoy it as an appetizer.

3 cups long rice cakes, sliced into 2-inch strips
  (available in Asian supermarkets)
½ teaspoon salt
1 tablespoon soy sauce
1 clove garlic, minced
¼ teaspoon ground white pepper, or to taste
2 tablespoons raw or brown sugar
½ pound shiitake or button mushrooms, sliced
½ pound lean ground beef
1 small onion, sliced thin (½ cup)
1 carrot, peeled and cut into 1-inch slivers
2 tablespoons sesame oil
1 tablespoon red pepper paste, or to taste
4 tablespoons beef broth
3 green onions, cut into 1-inch slivers

Add the rice cakes and salt to 1 quart boiling water. Cook for 7 to 8 minutes, or until tender. Rinse in cold water and drain thoroughly. Stir together the soy sauce, garlic, pepper, sugar, mushrooms, and beef. Add the beef mixture, onion, carrot, and oil to a wok or large skillet. Stir-fry for 8 to 9 minutes, or until the beef is done and the vegetables are tender.

Add the rice cakes, red pepper paste, and broth to the beef mixture. Simmer, stirring occasionally, for 3 minutes. Remove from heat. Add the green onions, cover, and allow the flavors to marry for 8 to 10 minutes.

YIELDS 6 SERVINGS.

Hint: Long rice cakes (*ttok*) may be stir-fried with a versatile mixture of vegetables: mushrooms, onions, carrots, bamboo shoots, or cucumbers. Use what is on hand and create a unique dish each time!

Rooster
AUTUMN

Metal Rooster

February 8, 1921 to January 27, 1922
February 5, 1981 to January 24, 1982

Clever and analytical,
be wary of becoming critical of others less gifted.

Auspicious Foods
Seafood, cookies, peaches, spicy flavors.

Chili Breast of Duck with Honey-Glazed Taro

2 pairs boneless duck breasts
1/2 teaspoon salt, or to taste
1/2 teaspoon pepper, or to taste
2 chili peppers, minced without seeds
1/2 cup honey
8 cloves garlic, minced
1/4 cup rice wine
1 quart chicken stock
1 tablespoon red pepper paste (ko chu jang), or to taste
2 cups peeled and diced taro root
2 teaspoons roasted sesame seeds
1/4 cup minced parsley

Preheat the oven to 350°F. Season the duck breasts with the salt, pepper, and chilies. Sear the duck breasts, skin side down, over medium heat for 5 to 6 minutes, or until golden brown. Pour off the drippings and set aside. Place the duck breasts in the oven. Bake for 12 to 15 minutes, or until medium rare. Reserving 2 tablespoons honey, drizzle the remainder of the honey over the duck while it bakes.

Sauté half the garlic in 1 tablespoon of the reserved drippings. Add the rice wine and chicken stock. Cook over high heat until reduced by half. Stir in the red pepper paste. Carefully transfer the duck breasts to the reduced stock and simmer gently for 5 to 7 minutes, or until the breasts are tender.

Parboil the taro for 3 to 4 minutes in 1 quart boiling water. Drain thoroughly and sauté the taro in a large skillet with 2 tablespoons duck drippings for 5 to 6 minutes, or until golden brown. Drain and add the reserved 2 tablespoons honey and remaining garlic, stirring to coat evenly.

Serve each duck breast on an individual platter. Drizzle several spoonfuls of the broth over each breast. Garnish with sesame seeds and parsley. Arrange the taro along one side of the plate.

YIELDS 4 SERVINGS.

Water Rooster

January 26, 1933 to February 13, 1934
January 23, 1993 to February 9, 1994

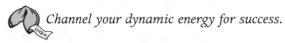 *Channel your dynamic energy for success.*

Auspicious Foods
Seafood, cookies, chestnuts, salty flavors.

Rice with Mixed Vegetables

BIBIM BAP

Bibim bap consists of a bowl of cooked rice mixed with assorted vegetables and meat. It is a festive dish because of the colorful ingredients. Traditionally five different colors are displayed: white, black, green, red, and yellow, the colors symbolizing the "Five Lucks." There is no nutritional need to include all five, but the multicolored presentation definitely adds eye appeal!

4 cups cooked rice
½ pound leftover Barbecued Beef Sirloin (see recipe page 96)
2 tablespoons brown sugar
½ teaspoon salt, or to taste
½ teaspoon ground black pepper, or to taste
1 carrot, peeled and quartered
½ cup spinach leaves, rinsed and patted dry
4 green onions, slivered
1 cucumber, cut into ½-inch by 2-inch lengths
1 zucchini, cut into ½-inch by 2-inch lengths
2 cups soy bean sprouts
8 shiitake mushrooms
3 tablespoons sesame oil
1 teaspoon soy sauce
4 eggs
½ cup sautéed bellflower root (page 151)

½ cup fern bracken (page 153)
1 teaspoon sesame seeds
½ cup red pepper paste

Heat the rice and beef separately. Combine the sugar, salt, and pepper. Distribute evenly among the carrots, spinach, green onions, cucumber, zucchini, sprouts, and mushrooms. Using 2 tablespoons of the oil, evenly distribute it among the vegetables. Stir-fry each vegetable separately, being careful to cook each only until tender-crisp. Do not overcook. Add the soy sauce to the mushrooms. Fry the eggs sunny-side up in the remaining 1 tablespoon of oil.

Equally distribute the rice among four bowls. Place the vegetables, then the bellflower root and bracken on top. Add the beef strips to this, and cover with a fried egg. Sprinkle with sesame seeds. Serve with the red pepper paste.

YIELDS 4 ENTRÉE SERVINGS.

Hint: To yield 8 side-dish servings, divide the rice, beef, and vegetables among 8 smaller bowls, increase the number of fried eggs to 8, and top each bowl with a fried egg.

Sautéed Bellflower Root

DORAJI NAMUL

1 cup dried bellflower root (available in Asian
   supermarkets)
1 ½ teaspoons salt, or to taste
3 cloves garlic, minced
¼ teaspoon ground white pepper
2 tablespoons sesame oil
1 teaspoon sugar
1 green onion, finely sliced
1 teaspoon sesame seeds

Allow the dried bellflower root to soak in water for 2 to 3 days. Keep refrigerated and change the water daily. Drain, slice off the ends, and cut into 2-inch strips. Sprinkle with 1 teaspoon salt. Blanch in boiling water for 1 minute. Remove, rinse in cold water, and drain thoroughly.

Sauté the bellflower root, garlic, and pepper in the sesame oil for 1 to 2 minutes. Add the remaining ½ teaspoon salt and the sugar. If necessary, add a tablespoon or two of water to prevent the bellflower root from scorching. Cook for 2 to 3 minutes, or until the vegetable is tender. Garnish with green onion and sesame seeds.

YIELDS 4 SERVINGS.

Bellflower Root Salad

Doraji Namul

Bellflower roots are the basis of this subtly flavored salad. The red pepper paste imparts not only flavor, but also a festive scarlet color.

> *4 ounces fresh bellflower root (available in Asian supermarkets) or 2 cups thinly sliced fresh jicama*
> *2 cloves garlic, minced*
> *6 green onions, julienned*
> *2 tablespoons rice wine vinegar*
> *2 tablespoons sugar*
> *2 tablespoons sesame oil*
> *2 teaspoons red pepper paste, or to taste (available in Asian supermarkets)*
> *1 teaspoon salt, or to taste*
> *1 teaspoon sesame seeds*

Slice off the ends of the bellflower root, peel, and tear or slice lengthwise into thin strips (about 2 cups). Except for the sesame seeds, combine all ingredients thoroughly, reserving several green onion strips. Divide the salad among four iced plates. Garnish with the remaining green onion strips, and sprinkle with sesame seeds.

YIELDS 4 SERVINGS.

Sautéed Fern Bracken

Buddhist monks or families living near the mountains pick the young spring shoots of fiddlehead ferns. The shoots are then par-boiled, dried, and stored for year-round use.

1 cup dried fern bracken
1 teaspoon brown sugar
1 tablespoon soy sauce
¼ teaspoon ground white pepper, or to taste
¼ pound ground beef
2 tablespoons sesame oil
3 cloves garlic, minced
4 sweet red peppers, seeded and sliced
2 tablespoons beef broth
4 green onions, slivered
1 teaspoon sesame seeds
½ teaspoon salt, or to taste
¼ teaspoon red pepper powder, optional (available in
    Asian supermarkets)

Soak the dried bracken in water in the refrigerator overnight. Remove and drain. Boil in 3 cups water for 1 hour. Remove, rinse under cold water, drain thoroughly, and slice into 2-inch pieces.

Marinate bracken in the sugar, soy sauce, and pepper for 1 hour. Combine the bracken, beef, oil, garlic, and peppers in a skillet or wok, and stir-fry for 4 to 5 minutes, or until the beef is cooked. Add the broth and green onions and simmer for 3 to 4 minutes, or until the liquid has been absorbed, and the bracken is tender.

Sprinkle with sesame seeds, salt, and red pepper powder and serve piping hot.

YIELDS 4 SERVINGS.

Wood Rooster

February 13, 1945 to February 1, 1946

A mild persona does not reflect
your innate strength and abilities.

Auspicious Foods
Seafood, cookies, heart of palm, sour flavors.

Sweet and Sour Tofu

TONG SU TUBU

4 cups firm tofu, cut into ½-inch cubes
½ cup sesame oil
1 cup diagonally sliced celery
1 cup red bell pepper, cut into ¼-inch strips
1 cup green bell pepper, cut into ¼-inch strips
8 green onions, diagonally sliced
2 cups fresh pea pods, ends and veins removed
2 chili peppers, minced, optional
1 cup vegetable broth
3 tablespoons cornstarch
½ cup soy sauce
6 tablespoons raw or white sugar
½ cup rice vinegar
6 to 8 cups steamed rice

Stir-fry the tofu and oil over a high flame in a wok for 2 to 3 minutes, or until the tofu is golden brown. Remove the tofu with a slotted spoon; keep warm.

Add the celery, peppers, onions, pea pods, and chili peppers to the wok. Stir-fry over high heat for 3 to 4 minutes. Spoon the tofu back into the wok. Mix the broth and cornstarch. Add to the wok, along with the soy sauce, sugar, and rice vinegar. Cook the mixture over low heat, stirring occasionally for 2 to 3 minutes, or until it thickens. Serve over steamed rice.

YIELDS 8 SERVINGS.

Hint: Recipe may be halved.

Mung Bean Sprouts Salad

SUKJU NAMUL

Like soy bean sprouts, mung bean sprouts can be grown indoors without sun or soil.

2 cups blanched, chilled mung bean sprouts
2 tablespoons sesame oil
1 clove garlic, minced
2 tablespoons soy sauce
2 teaspoons toasted sesame seeds

Combine all the ingredients except the sesame seeds. Toss lightly to cover. Divide among 4 frosty salad plates, and sprinkle with the sesame seeds.

YIELDS 4 SERVINGS.

Fire Rooster

January 31, 1957 to February 17, 1958

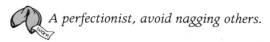 *A perfectionist, avoid nagging others.*

Auspicious Foods
Seafood, cookies, almonds, bitter flavors.

Almond Cookies

1 cup butter
¾ cup sugar
3 eggs
1 tablespoon almond extract
2 ¼ cups flour, sifted
½ teaspoon baking soda
¼ teaspoon salt
½ cup blanched almond halves

Cream the butter and sugar. Beat in 2 of the eggs, one at a time, mixing well. Blend in the almond extract.

In another bowl, combine the flour, baking soda, and salt. Gradually fold the flour mixture into the shortening. The dough should be fairly firm. Divide the dough in half and roll each into a cylinder, about 1 ½ inches in diameter. Wrap in waxed paper and refrigerate for at least 4 hours.

Preheat the oven to 375°F. Cut the dough crosswise into ¼-inch slices. Arrange cookies on an ungreased cookie sheet. Top each cookie with an almond half. Beat remaining egg and brush cookies lightly with it. Bake for about 10 minutes, or until light golden brown.

YIELDS 2 DOZEN.

Earth Rooster

February 17, 1969 to February 05, 1970

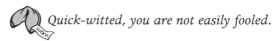 *Quick-witted, you are not easily fooled.*

Auspicious Foods
Seafood, cookies, sweet flavors.

Sweet Anchovy Condiment

MARUN PANCHAN

> 2 teaspoons sesame oil
> 1 tablespoon brown sugar
> 1 teaspoon soy sauce
> 1 garlic clove, minced
> $\frac{1}{4}$-inch slice fresh ginger, minced
> $\frac{1}{2}$ teaspoon ko chu jang *(available in Asian supermarkets)*
>   or $\frac{1}{4}$ teaspoon chili pepper, or to taste
> 1 cup dried anchovies
> 2 teaspoons toasted sesame seeds

Heat the sesame oil in a wok or skillet. Add the sugar, soy sauce, garlic, ginger and *ko chu jang*. Stir-fry over low heat for 1 minute, or until the mixture begins to bubble.

Rapidly fold in the anchovies for 30 seconds, being sure to coat the anchovies evenly. Remove from the heat, stir in the sesame seeds, and present in a rice bowl. Serve chilled or at room temperature.

YIELDS 1 $\frac{1}{2}$ CUPS.

BETWEEN SEASONS

Dog

Metal Dog

February 10, 1910 to January 29, 1911
February 6, 1970 to January 26, 1971

To fulfill your dreams, beware of distractions and impatience.

Auspicious Foods
Rice dishes, congee, peaches, spicy flavors.

Crispy Lotus Root

1 pound lotus root (available in Asian supermarkets)
1 cup wheat flour
1/2 cup potato flour or wheat flour
1/4 pound ground beef
1/2 teaspoon salt, or to taste
1/8 teaspoon ground black pepper, or to taste
1 clove garlic, minced
3 cups vegetable oil
1 egg, lightly beaten

Rinse the lotus root and cut in half lengthwise. Soak in 1 quart salted water for 5 to 10 minutes, remove, drain, and pat dry. Combine the flours. Lightly dust the 2 cut surfaces of the lotus root with 1 tablespoon of the flour mixture.

Combine the beef with 1/4 teaspoon salt, the pepper, and garlic. Spread the beef mixture evenly over the cut surfaces of the lotus root. Press the two halves together. Carefully slice the cylinder into

½-inch rounds. Place the oil in a wok or deep-fry pan. Bring the temperature to 350°F.

Combine the remaining flour, ¼ teaspoon salt, and the egg with ¾ cup water. Stir briskly to form a thin batter. Dip each lotus root slice in the mixture to lightly coat. Using tongs or a slotted spoon, carefully lower each round into the hot oil. Deep-fry for 1 to 2 minutes, or until golden brown. Carefully remove the lotus-root rounds from the oil and drain on paper towels. Serve piping hot.

YIELDS 2 DOZEN.

Water Dog

January 28, 1922 to February 15, 1923
January 25, 1982 to February 12, 1983

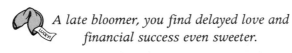 *A late bloomer, you find delayed love and financial success even sweeter.*

Auspicious Foods
Rice dishes, congee, chestnuts, salty flavors.

Fried Rice

BOKKEUMBAP

Fried rice is the consummate answer to leftovers. The dish has no specific recipe or ingredients. In fact, it's never made the same way twice. Use whatever is on hand. Chop up almost any bit of meat, fish, or vegetable, and add it to the recipe, even day-old rice. Top with a fried egg, sunny-side up, and you have a traditional Korean meal!

3 tablespoons sesame oil
1 clove garlic, minced
4 green onions, thinly sliced
¼ cup diced mushrooms
½ teaspoon salt, or to taste
¼ teaspoon ground white pepper, or to taste
1 tablespoon soy sauce, or to taste
1 cup finely chopped cooked meat or shellfish
4 cups steamed rice
4 eggs
1 tablespoon fresh cilantro leaves

Combine 2 tablespoons oil, garlic, onions, mushrooms, salt, pepper, and soy sauce in a wok. Stir-fry over medium heat for 2 to 3 minutes. Add the meat or shellfish and rice. Stir-fry for 2 to 3 minutes, or until heated through, adding a tablespoon of water if mixture begins to stick to the wok. Spoon into 4 large bowls. Fry the eggs sunny-side up in the remaining 1 tablespoon oil, and carefully place on top of the fried rice. Garnish with cilantro leaves and serve at once.

YIELDS 4 SERVINGS.

Alternatives: Add bits of any cut of beef, pork, bacon, ham, lamb, chicken, duck, tofu, shrimp, clams, fish, crabmeat, lobster, scallops, squid, eggs, green pepper, red pepper, zucchini, napa cabbage, peas, pea pods, celery, corn, carrots, onions, leeks, chives, bean sprouts, bamboo shoots, grated ginger, or chili pepper.

Stir-Fried Octopus

NAKJI BOKKEUMBAP

Use 1 cup octopus, cut into bite-sized pieces, in lieu of the cooked meat or shellfish in the Fried Rice recipe above. Add $\frac{1}{4}$ teaspoon chili pepper to the ingredients. Stir-fry the octopus with the chili pepper, vegetables, and other seasonings for 3 to 4 minutes, or until the octopus turns an opaque white color. Continue to follow the directions for the Fried Rice.

YIELDS 4 SERVINGS.

Bean Sprout Salad

$\frac{1}{4}$ cup sesame oil
$\frac{1}{4}$ cup vinegar
$\frac{1}{4}$ cup soy sauce
$\frac{1}{2}$ teaspoon salt, or to taste
$\frac{1}{4}$ teaspoon pepper
$\frac{1}{4}$ cup finely chopped green onion
$\frac{1}{4}$ cup thinly sliced sweet red pepper
$\frac{1}{4}$ cup sesame seeds
1 clove garlic, minced
2 cups mung bean sprouts

Combine the oil, vinegar, soy sauce, salt, pepper, green onion, red pepper, sesame seeds, and garlic in a covered glass jar.

Keep the bean sprouts cool until ready to serve. Shake the jar of dressing. Combine the dressing and the bean sprouts in a large wooden salad bowl. Toss gently and serve.

Yields 4 servings.

Wood Dog

February 14, 1934 to February 3, 1935
February 10, 1994 to January 30, 1995

 A born hero and romantic, you are an all-around success.

Auspicious Foods
Rice dishes, congee, heart of palm, sour flavors.

Radish Cube Kimchi

KKAKTTUGI

Kkakttugi is made from daikon (white radish) cubes mixed with spices and seasonings. Add mustard leaves or the inner leaves of cabbage for variety. Salted shrimp lends a piquant flavor to this kimchi.

> *1 pound daikon (white radish)*
> *2 tablespoons salt*
> *1 cup fresh mugwort*
> *2 tablespoons red chili pepper powder, or to taste*
> *9 cloves garlic, minced*
> *1 tablespoon minced fresh ginger*
> *9 green onions, julienned*
> *2 tablespoons brown sugar*
> *1 tablespoon dried salted shrimp (available in Asian supermarkets)*

Peel the daikon and cut into ¾-inch cubes. Soak in 1 quart water with 1 tablespoon salt for 20 minutes. Wash and trim the mugwort. Cut in 1-inch-long pieces.

Drain the daikon and toss with the red chili pepper powder until evenly coated. Add 1 tablespoon salt and the remaining ingredients. Mix well and place the mixture in a kimchi crock or large glass jar. Cover and allow to ferment for 2 days at room temperature. Use immediately or refrigerate remaining kimchi.

YIELDS 1 QUART.

Fire Dog

February 2, 1946 to January 21, 1947

*With your talents and abilities,
don't settle; succeed.*

Auspicious Foods
Rice dishes, congee, almonds, bitter flavors.

Korean Barbecued Short Ribs

KALBI GUI

1 tablespoon toasted sesame seeds
1 cup soy sauce
¼ cup sweet rice wine or sherry
½ cup brown sugar
2 large pears, peeled, cored, and coarsely chopped
1 tablespoon finely minced fresh ginger
. 4 garlic cloves, minced
1 tablespoon dried chili peppers, crumbled, or to taste
6 pounds beef short ribs, cut into 2 ½-inch lengths

Combine the sesame seeds, soy sauce, wine, sugar, pears, ginger, garlic, and chili peppers. Place the ribs in a large plastic bag. Pour the marinade over the ribs, pressing air out of bag and sealing securely. Marinate overnight in the refrigerator. Keep the ribs chilled until ready to grill.

Remove the ribs from the bag, shaking off any excess marinade. Grill the ribs over hot coals, turning and basting, for 15 to 18 minutes, or until the ribs are brown and crisp.

YIELDS 4 SERVINGS.

Earth Dog

February 18, 1958 to February 7, 1959

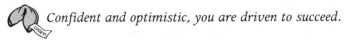 *Confident and optimistic, you are driven to succeed.*

Auspicious Foods
Rice dishes, congee, dates, sweet flavors.

Sesame Pumpkin-Seed Brittle

TONG KKAE

Sesame seeds are an integral part of Korean cookery. Roasted whole sesame seeds are used for candy and garnishes. However, the flavor of crushed seeds is more pungent, so ground sesame seeds are the more popular seasoning.

½ teaspoon sesame oil
2 cups raw or light brown sugar
½ cup hulled green pumpkin seeds
¼ cup roasted sesame seeds

Line a cookie sheet with foil. Lightly grease the foil with sesame oil. Caramelize the sugar in a heavy skillet by stirring with a fork over medium heat until the sugar has melted and become a golden caramel. Be very careful when working with hot candy! Remove the skillet from the heat, and add the pumpkin and sesame seeds. Working quickly, pour the mixture onto the foiled pan. After the brittle cools, break it into bite-sized pieces.

YIELDS **8** SERVINGS.

Cream of Pine Nut Bisque

JAT JUK

Save room for this warm and creamy after-dinner dessert soup!

> 9 dried jujubes (Korean dates; available in Asian
>   supermarkets)
> 2 tablespoons honey
> 1 cup pine nuts
> $\frac{1}{2}$ cup rice flour
> 1 teaspoon sugar
> $\frac{1}{4}$ teaspoon salt

Rehydrate the jujubes in 2 cups water for 2 hours. Drain and remove the pits. Slice the jujubes thinly and coat lightly with honey.

Using the pulse setting of a food processor, grind the pine nuts with 1 cup water for 1 minute. Force the mixture through a tea strainer, using the back of a wooden spoon.

In a small saucepan, combine the flour with 1 cup water. Simmer over a low flame, stirring constantly for 5 minutes, or until the mixture begins to bubble and thicken.

Fold in the pine-nut mixture along with the sugar and salt. Stir continuously until just before it comes to a boil. Remove the soup from the heat, ladle it into elegant rice bowls, and garnish with honeyed jujubes.

YIELDS 8 SERVINGS.

Boar
WINTER

Metal Boar

January 30, 1911 to February 17, 1912
January 27, 1971 to February 15, 1972

Open-minded and warm-hearted, you are surrounded by friends.

Auspicious Foods
Soup, Oolong tea, candied ginger, peaches, spicy flavors.

Grilled Chicken on a Skewer

KKOCHI GUI

These skewers include grape tomatoes—sweet tomatoes about the size of grapes. These are considered a fruit in Korea, not a vegetable, and are sweet enough to be eaten for dessert. However, used in cooking, their natural sugars add another dimension, subtly enhancing the flavors of the chicken and peppers.

For added flavor (and easy cleanup), use fresh sprigs of mugwort instead of a brush to apply the sauce.

> *1 pound boneless chicken breast*
> *4 small onions, halved*
> *1 green bell pepper*
> *1 sweet yellow pepper*
> *2 sweet red peppers*
> *8 grape tomatoes or cherry tomatoes*
> *¹/₂ cup soy sauce*

2 tablespoons molasses
2 tablespoons rice wine
2 tablespoons sesame oil
2 teaspoons mustard
Mugwort sprigs, optional

Remove the skin from the chicken. Cut into 1 by 1 $\frac{1}{2}$ by $\frac{1}{2}$ -inch pieces. Peel onions and slice in half. Remove stems and seeds from peppers. Cut each pepper into 8 large squares. Except for the mugwort sprigs, combine the remaining ingredients, blending thoroughly.

Thread the chicken cubes, pepper chunks, onion halves, and whole tomatoes onto four 18-inch skewers, alternating ingredients, colors, and textures. Brush liberally with the sauce. Grill, turning occasionally, for 10 to 12 minutes, or until the vegetables are tender and the chicken is done (no pink is visible when the chicken is pierced with a fork).

YIELDS 4 SERVINGS.

Alternative: Cut the chicken, onion, and peppers into $\frac{1}{2}$ by $\frac{3}{4}$ by $\frac{1}{4}$-inch pieces (half the size mentioned above). Thread the ingredients onto 8-inch cocktail skewers. Brush with sauce and grill for 5 to 6 minutes, or until the vegetables are tender and the chicken is done (no pink is visible when the chicken is pierced with a fork).

YIELDS 12 COCKTAIL SKEWERS.

Water Boar

February 16, 1923 to February 23,1924
February 13, 1983 to February 1, 1984

 Responsibility and prudence lead to success.

Auspicious Foods
Soup, Oolong tea, candied ginger, chestnuts, salty flavors.

Seaweed Soup

MIYOK KUK

Because of its nutritional value, seaweed soup is given the attribute of long life and is eaten each birthday until a person is 60 years old. High in calcium and iodine, low in cholesterol, seaweed soup is believed to purify the blood and improve the complexion.

2 cups dried seaweed (available in Asian supermarkets)
¼ cup sesame oil
½ pound chuck beef
1 teaspoon soy sauce
6 cups beef broth
2 dozen mussels
½ teaspoon salt, or to taste
¼ teaspoon ground black pepper, or to taste
½ teaspoon sesame seeds

Cut the seaweed into 1-inch strips. Cover with cold water and allow to rehydrate for ½ hour. Squeeze out excess water. Drain thoroughly. Stir-fry the seaweed in the oil over medium heat for 5 to 6 minutes.

Thinly slice the beef into 1-inch strips. Add the beef, soy sauce, and ½ cup of broth to the wok. Cover and braise for 3 to 4 minutes. Add the remaining 5 ½ cups broth. Bring to a boil, then lower the heat, cover, and simmer for 15 minutes.

Scrub and rinse the mussels. Uncover the soup, and again bring to a rolling boil. Carefully add the mussels with a slotted spoon. Boil for 5 minutes or until the mussel shells open. Season with salt and pepper. Garnish with the sesame seeds. Serve steaming hot.

YIELDS 8 CUPS OR 4 LARGE BOWLS.

Wood Boar

February 4, 1935 to January 23, 1936
January 31, 1995 to February 18, 1996

 You are generous to a fault.

Auspicious Foods
Soup, Oolong tea, candied ginger, heart of palm, sour flavors.

Instant Kimchi

MAK KIMCHI

1 small head napa cabbage
6 green onions, thinly sliced diagonally
½ teaspoon red pepper powder, or to taste
1 teaspoon grated ginger
1 clove garlic, finely minced
3 tablespoons sesame oil
3 tablespoons rice wine vinegar
2 tablespoons soy sauce, or to taste
2 teaspoons toasted sesame seeds

Tear the cabbage into bite-sized pieces. Toss lightly in a large bowl
with the green onions. In a small bowl, combine the red pepper
powder, ginger, garlic, sesame oil, vinegar, and soy sauce. Pour
over greens and toss until the greens are lightly coated. Garnish
with sesame seeds, and serve immediately.

YIELDS 4 TO 6 SERVINGS.

Layered Beef and Cabbage Pie

2 pounds (1 large head) cabbage leaves
1 pound ground beef
1 pound ground pork
$\frac{1}{2}$ cup thinly sliced green onion
4 cloves garlic, minced
3 tablespoons soy sauce
$\frac{1}{2}$ cup plus 1 tablespoon potato flour or wheat flour
3 tablespoons sesame oil
3 tablespoons raw or brown sugar
$\frac{1}{4}$ teaspoon cayenne pepper, or to taste
$\frac{1}{2}$ cup coarsely chopped sweet red pepper
$\frac{1}{2}$ cup coarsely chopped bell pepper
1 cup canned corn, drained
1 tablespoon rice vinegar
$\frac{1}{2}$ cup sliced shiitake mushrooms

Preheat the oven to 350°F. Blanch the cabbage in boiling water. Remove and drain. When it is cool enough to handle, separate the leaves and pat dry. Combine the beef, pork, green onion, garlic, soy sauce, $\frac{1}{2}$ cup flour, sesame oil, 1 tablespoon sugar, cayenne, red and bell peppers, and $\frac{1}{2}$ cup corn.

Lightly oil a deep-dish pie pan or ovenproof bowl. Line the container with cabbage leaves. Place a small amount of the meat mixture on top. Cover with another layer of cabbage leaves and continue layering with the remaining meat and cabbage, ending with a top layer of cabbage leaves. Sprinkle with 1 tablespoon water and bake for 45 minutes, or until the pork is thoroughly cooked.

While the mixture is baking, add 2 cups water with the remaining 2 tablespoons sugar, $\frac{1}{2}$ cup corn, the vinegar, and mushrooms to a 2-quart pan. Bring to a boil, and then lower to a simmer. Combine 2 tablespoons cool water with the remaining 1 tablespoon flour. Stir until smooth. Gradually add the flour mixture to the sauce, stirring constantly. Add 1 tablespoon more water if necessary.

Remove the beef and cabbage tart from the oven. When cool enough to handle, carefully invert the pan over a platter. Remove the pie pan. Drain any excess juice. Spoon the sauce over all, and slice into 8 wedges.

YIELDS 8 SERVINGS.

Fire Boar

January 22, 1947 to February 9, 1948

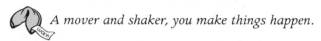 *A mover and shaker, you make things happen.*

Auspicious Foods
Soup, Oolong tea, candied ginger, almonds, bitter flavors.

Spiced Mushrooms

BEUSEUS DOEN JANG JEEGE

Doen jang is a popular Korean seasoning made from steamed and fermented soybeans. It is used primarily as a flavoring for dipping sauces and stews.

> *30 dried mushrooms*
> *6 tablespoons* doen jang *soybean paste (available in Asian supermarkets)*
> *12 cloves garlic, minced*
> *18 green onions, cut into 1-inch lengths*

Rinse the mushrooms and cover with 3 cups water. Allow to steep for 1 hour, or until softened. Shred the mushroom caps into thin slices, discarding the stems. Reserve the liquid, adding more water, if necessary, to make 3 cups.

Bring the liquid and *doen jang* bean paste to a boil in a 2-quart pot. Lower heat and simmer, covered, for 8 to 10 minutes, or until the bean paste has dissolved. Add the mushrooms, garlic, and green onions. Bring to a boil again and simmer for 5 to 6 minutes. Serve warm over rice.

YIELDS 4 TO 6 SERVINGS.

Steamed Asparagus

Check the asparagus carefully when purchasing. The tips should be compact, not flowered. The stalks should be firm, with a deep green color. The bottoms have an inch or two of woody base, which must be trimmed before cooking.

2 pounds fresh asparagus, or 6 to 8 stalks per person
Salted boiling water

Break off (do not cut) the woody base from each asparagus stalk. The woody bases will snap off from the tender portions. Wash stalks thoroughly under running cold water.

Tie the stalks into serving-sized bunches. Stand upright in a deep saucepan that contains an inch of salted, boiling water. Cover and allow to steam for 13 to 15 minutes, or until the asparagus is tender but crisp.

YIELDS 4 SERVINGS

Earth Boar

February 8, 1959 to January 27, 1960

 You achieve success the old-fashioned way: you earn it.

Auspicious Foods
Soup, Oolong tea, candied ginger, dates, sweet flavors.

Crescent Rice Cakes

SONGP'YON

These crescent-shaped rice cakes are a special dessert prepared for holidays. Make them a day ahead, and store them in the refrigerator. You will need wet cloths (thicker than cheesecloth) for this recipe.

> 3 cups rice flour
> 1 ½ cups sesame seeds, roasted
> 1 cup raw sugar or light brown sugar
> ½ teaspoon salt, or to taste
> 1 cup pine needles, washed
> 2 tablespoons sesame oil

Add ¾ cup water to rice flour, adding another tablespoon or two, if necessary, to make a stiff dough. Knead the dough only until the flour and water hold together. Cover the dough with a wet cloth.

Combine the sesame seeds, sugar, and salt for the filling. Tear off a 1-inch piece of rice dough and roll into a ball between your hands. Press your thumb into the ball to create a hole. Place 1 teaspoon sesame-seed filling into the cavity and stretch the rice dough to completely cover the filling. If necessary, dampen your fingers to make the dough stick together. Create a round or crescent shape.

Using a double boiler or steamer, bring 2 quarts water to a boil.

Line the steamer with a wet cloth. Arrange the *songp'yon* on top. Scatter the pine needles over all. Then layer another wet cloth over this. Steam the *songp'yon* for 35 to 40 minutes, or until they are tender and a bit transparent. Remove them from the steamer, rinse with cold water, drain, and brush them lightly with sesame oil.

YIELDS ABOUT 36.

Index